Armstrong on Reinventing Performance Management

Armstrong on Reinventing Performance Management

Building a culture of continuous improvement

Michael Armstrong

First published in Great Britain and the United States in 2017 by Kogan Page Limited

2nd Floor, 45 Gee Street	c/o Martin P Hill Consulting	4737/23 Ansari Road
London	122 W 27th St, 10th Floor	Daryaganj
EC1V 3RS	New York, NY 10001	New Delhi 110002
United Kingdom	USA	India

www.koganpage.com

© Michael Armstrong, 2017

ISBN   978 0 7494 7811 7
E-ISBN   978 0 7494 7812 4

British Library Cataloguing-in-Publication Data

A CIP record for this book is available from the British Library.

Library of Congress Cataloging-in-Publication Data

Names: Armstrong, Michael, 1928- author.
Title: Armstrong on reinventing performance management : building a culture
   of continuous improvement / Michael Armstrong.
Description: London ; New York : Kogan Page, 2017. | Includes index.
Identifiers: LCCN 2016039576 (print) | LCCN 2016053475 (ebook) | ISBN
   9780749478117 (pbk.) | ISBN 9780749478124 (ebook)
Subjects: LCSH: Personnel management.
Classification: LCC HF5549 .A89759 2017 (print) | LCC HF5549 (ebook) | DDC
   658.3/12–dc23
LC record available at
https://lccn.loc.gov/2016039576

Typeset by Integra Software Services, Pondicherry
Print production managed by Jellyfish
Printed and bound by CPI Group (UK) Ltd, Croydon CR0 4YY

CONTENTS

Introduction

Performance management is broken. It is supposed to enhance organizational performance by improving individual and team performance but it doesn't. It starts off with good intentions but they fail to materialize. Managers don't like doing it and if they try they tend to do it badly. Employees feel that it is both unfair and irrelevant. HR people despair because their pet project is clearly not working. Everyone is bogged down in the bureaucracy of forms, ratings and formal reviews.

Perhaps the following observations by Professor Samuel Colbert of the UCLA Anderson School of Management are a bit over the top, but they ring true:

> This corporate sham is one of the most insidious, most damaging, and yet most ubiquitous of corporate activities. Everybody does it and almost everyone who has been evaluated hates it. It's a pretentious, bogus practice that produces absolutely nothing that any thinking executive should call a corporate plus.
>
> (Colbert, 2010)

Hostile views such as these have multiplied. Most have focused on a number of performance management features that have contributed to the problem of getting it to work, including the reluctance or inability of line managers to carry out their performance management responsibilities as required. These features comprise:

- The emphasis on an annual formal review and the consequential neglect of performance management activities such as providing feedback during the rest of the year.

- The practice of looking backwards at what had or had not been achieved rather than forward to what should and could be achieved.

- An over-emphasis on superficial top-down judgements expressed as ratings.

- The use of forced distribution rating systems.
- The direct link to pay decisions that diverted attention from the developmental nature of performance management, which should be its most important feature.
- An over-bureaucratic approach involving the use of elaborate forms and procedures.
- A tendency for the system to be owned by HR rather than by the line managers to whom it properly belongs.

Over the years people like Duncan Brown and Helen Murlis and many other commentators, including myself, have been making these criticisms, but they have largely been voices crying in the wilderness. However, there has recently been a surge of opinion expressing the belief that something needs to be done and a number of large organizations have announced significant changes. This is perhaps because of the cumulative impact of all that has been written but also because many businesses (called post-bureaucratic organizations by Jonathan Trevor of Cambridge University) are operating much more flexibly and therefore reject the bureaucratic system that performance management can too easily become.

The groundswell of opinion – and practice – indicates a significant shift away from traditional performance management/appraisal practices: performance management is being reinvented. This move focuses on replacing the formal annual performance review with more frequent and less formal discussion/feedback sessions, an abolition of ratings, especially forced distribution systems, decoupling performance review from performance pay decisions and more emphasis on continuous development (forward rather than backward looking).

The following observations on what is happening to performance management were made recently by the accountants and management consultants Deloitte (2015):

> Innovative new performance management models are now becoming an imperative as businesses modernize and improve their talent solutions. Companies leading this transformation are redefining the way they set goals and evaluate performance, focusing heavily on coaching and feedback and looking for new technologies to help make performance management easier.

Today's organizations should closely examine their performance processes and push toward simplification and strengths-based assessment and coaching. The days of traditional appraisals and forced ranking are coming to an end; performance management is now a tool for greater employee engagement.

An article in the September 2015 edition of *People Management* titled 'Appraisals are finished: what's next?' summarizes this view, albeit melodramatically. It refers to the following firms that have recently made significant changes: Accenture, Deloitte (United States), Expedia, Facebook, Gap, Microsoft and Netflix.

Clearly there is a need to rethink how performance management operates. It needs to be reinvented. And that is the theme of this book. The starting point is an analysis of the concept of performance management – how it is supposed to work. The reality of how it actually does work is explored next and consideration is given to the ways in which, ideally, performance management should function. The practices of firms that have recently reinvented performance management will be described; comprehensive case studies prepared by e-reward (2016) of what Gap and Microsoft have done are set out in the Appendices. The rest of the book is devoted to reviewing the issues involved and examining what can be done in the major aspects of performance management, namely: objective setting, the annual performance review, rating and ranking, personal development, the provision of training and the reinvention programme. The conclusion reached is that performance management should not only be reinvented, it should also be renamed 'performance and development', as at Microsoft, to recognize that its purpose is to develop performance, not simply to manage it.

References

Colbert, S A (2010) *Get Rid of the Performance Review*, Hachette, New York
Deloitte (2015) www2.deloitte.com/uk/en/../performance-management-redesign-human-capital-trends-2015.htm (accessed 10 May 2016)
e-reward (2016) *Performance Management Case Studies*, e-reward, Stockport

Performance management – the concept

01

Over the years a model of performance management has emerged. As described in this chapter it is conceptual in the sense that it is an abstract version of reality. The reality is examined in Chapter 2.

This chapter is divided into three parts. In the first, performance management is defined; the second part consists of a short history of performance management, which explains the background to the main features of performance management as described in the third part.

Performance management defined

Conceptually, performance management is a systematic process for improving organizational performance by developing the performance of individuals and teams. It is a means of getting better results by understanding and managing performance within an agreed framework of planned goals, standards and competency requirements.

A short history of performance management

According to Koontz (1971), the first known example of performance appraisal took place during the Wei dynasty (AD 221–265) when the emperor employed an 'imperial rater' whose task it was to evaluate the performance of the official family. In the 16th century Ignatius Loyola established a system for formal rating of the members of the Jesuit Society.

The first formal monitoring systems, however, evolved out of the work of Frederick Taylor and his followers before World War I. Rating for officers in the US armed services was introduced in the 1920s and this spread to the United Kingdom, as did some of the factory-based US systems. Merit rating came to the fore in the United States and the United Kingdom in the 1950s; in the 1960s it was renamed 'performance appraisal'. Management by objectives then came and largely went in the 1960s and '70s and, simultaneously, experiments were made with assessment techniques such as behaviourally anchored rating scales. A revised form of results-oriented performance appraisal emerged in the 1970s and still exists today. The term 'performance management' was first used in the 1970s but it did not become a recognized process until the latter half of the 1980s.

Merit rating

Merit rating was the process of assessing how well someone was regarded in terms of personality traits such as judgement or integrity and qualities such as leadership or cooperativeness. The term 'merit' recalled classroom judgements made by teachers. Merit rating often involved the quantification of judgements against each factor, presumably in the belief that the quantification of subjective judgements made them more objective.

W D Scott was the US pioneer who introduced rating of the abilities of workers in industry prior to World War I. He was very much influenced by F W Taylor (1911) and invented the 'Man to man comparison' scale, which was Taylorism in action. Many of the developments that followed, even to this day, are a form of Taylorism, which is F W Taylor's concept of scientific management, meaning the use of systematic observation and measurement, task specialism and, in effect, the reduction of workers to the level of efficiently functioning machines.

The W D Scott scale was modified and used to rate the efficiency of US army officers. It is said to have supplanted the seniority system of promotion in the army and initiated an era of promotion on the basis of merit. The perceived success of this system led to its adoption by the British Army.

Table 1.1 Example of a 'tick box' assessment

Consider his success in winning confidence and respect through his personality:

(a) inspiring ☐	(b) favourable ☐	(c) indifferent ☐
(d) unfavourable ☐	(e) repellent ☐	

The pioneering efforts of Scott were developed in the 1920s and '30s into what was termed the Graphic Rating Scale, used for reports on workers and rating managers and supervisors. A typical manager's or supervisor's scale included 'tick box' assessments of various qualities, like the example shown in Table 1.1. Times have changed.

The justification for the use of this sort of scale was that ratings were 'educational'. They ensured, it was said, that those making the reports analysed subordinates in terms of the traits essential for success in their work. The educational impact on employees was described as imparting the knowledge that they were being judged periodically on vital and important traits.

The original scale was said to have been based on thorough research by W D Scott and colleagues into what were the key criteria for rating people at work. The principle of the scale and the factors used were seized on with enthusiasm by organizations on both sides of the Atlantic as merit rating or, later, performance appraisal, flourished. This was without any research and analysis of the extent to which the factors were relevant (or whether dubbing someone as 'repellent' was a good idea). Surveys conducted by the CIPD (Armstrong and Baron, 1998; 2005) and e-reward (2004) revealed that there are organizations still using lists of competencies that include items that look suspiciously like some of the traits identified 70 years or more ago. They seemed to have been lifted down from some shelf (or extracted from a 'dictionary of competencies') without any research into the extent to which they were appropriate in the context of the organization. Merit rating still exists in some quarters even if it is now called 'performance management'.

Some companies use the total merit score as the basis for ranking employees and this is translated into a forced distribution for performance pay purposes; for example, the top 10 per cent in the ranking get a 5 per cent increase, the next 20 per cent a 4 per cent increase, and so on. To iron out rating inconsistencies one manufacturing company used a diabolical device it called 'factorizing'. This meant producing an average score for the whole company and amending the allocation of points in each department to ensure that their scores corresponded with the company average. As can be imagined, line managers did not take kindly to the implication that there were no differences between departmental performances.

The term 'merit rating' gradually morphed into 'performance appraisal' during the 1950s although it was usually only a change in name, not in content. 'Performance appraisal' is still used in some quarters as a generic term for performance management although, strictly speaking, it only refers to the review, assessment and rating aspects of performance management.

Attacks on merit rating and performance appraisal

Although merit rating in different guises still persists, a strong attack on the practice was mounted some time ago by Harvard professor Douglas McGregor in his *Harvard Business Review* article 'An uneasy look at performance appraisal' (1957).

McGregor on performance appraisal

The emphasis should be shifted from appraisal to analysis. This implies a more positive approach. No longer is the subordinate being examined by his superior so that his weaknesses may be determined; rather he is examining himself, in order to define not only his weaknesses but also his strengths and potentials… He becomes an active agent, not a passive 'object'. He is no longer a pawn in a chess game called management development.

McGregor went on to propose that the focus should be on the future rather than the past in order to establish realistic targets and to seek the most effective ways of reaching them. The accent of the review is therefore on performance, on actions relative to goals:

There is less a tendency for the personality of the subordinate to become an issue. The superior, instead of finding himself in the position of a psychologist or a therapist, can become a coach helping a subordinate to reach his own decisions on the specific steps that will enable him to reach his targets.

(McGregor, 1957)

In short, the main factor in the management of individual performance should be the analysis of the behaviour required to achieve agreed results, not the assessment of personality. This is partly management by objectives, which is concerned with planning and measuring results in relation to agreed targets and standards, but indicates that individual performance is about behaviour as well as results (a notion that management by objectives ignored). Douglas McGregor was way ahead of his time. His suggestions have been ignored continuously, right up to the present day.

A research project conducted by Kay Rowe (1964) in the United Kingdom came to broadly the same conclusion as McGregor – that managers do not like 'playing at being God' in rating the personalities of their subordinates:

Managers admitted they were hesitant (to appraise) because what they wrote might be misunderstood, because they might unduly affect a subordinate's future career, because they could only write what they were prepared to say and so on.

One comment made to Rowe was that: 'You feel rather like a schoolmaster writing an end-of-term report.' Rowe's conclusions were that:

- Appraisers were reluctant to appraise.
- The follow-up was inadequate.
- No attempt should be made to clarify or categorize performance in terms of grades. The difficulty of achieving common standards and the reluctance of appraisers to use the whole scale made them of little use.

These comments, especially the last one, are as relevant today as they were when they were made. Commentators are still producing these precepts as original truths. It is remarkable how much reinventing the wheel goes on in the field of performance management.

The attack on merit rating or the earlier versions of performance appraisal, as it came to be known in the 1960s, was often made on the grounds that it was mainly concerned with the assessment of traits. These could refer to the extent to which individuals were conscientious, imaginative, self-sufficient, cooperative, or possessed qualities of judgement, initiative, vigour or original thinking. The belief that trait behaviour is independent of situations (the work system) and the people with whom an individual is interacting is questionable. Trait measures cannot predict how a person will respond in a particular situation, and there is the problem of how anyone can be certain that someone has such and such a trait. Assessments of traits are only too likely to be prompted by subjective judgements and prejudices.

Management by objectives

The management by objectives movement claimed that it overcame the problems of trait rating. The term 'management by objectives' was first coined by Peter Drucker (1955).

Peter Drucker on management by objectives

What the business enterprise needs is a principle of management that will give full scope to individual strength and responsibility and at the same time give common direction of vision and effort, establish teamwork and harmonize the goals of the individual with the common weal. The only principle that can do this is management by objectives and self-control.

Drucker emphasized that 'an effective management must direct the vision and efforts of all managers towards a common goal'. This would ensure that individual and corporate objectives are integrated and would also make it possible for managers to control their own performance: 'Self-control means stronger motivation: a desire to do the best rather than just enough to get by. It means higher performance goals and broader vision.'

Douglas McGregor's (1960) contribution arose from his 'Theory Y' concept. He wrote: 'The central principle which derives from Theory Y is that of integration: the creation of conditions such that the members of the organization can achieve their own goals *best* by directing their efforts towards the success of the organization.' This is McGregor's principle of 'management by integration and self-control', which he insisted should be regarded as a strategy – a way of managing people.

Douglas McGregor on the principle of integration and self-control

The tactics are worked out in the light of the circumstances. Forms and procedures are of little value... 'selling' management a programme of target setting and providing standardized forms and procedures is the surest way to *prevent* the development of management by integration and self-control.

This principle may not have entered the vocabulary of performance management but is fully absorbed into current thinking about it. Many writers and management consultants recycle McGregor's philosophy without ever acknowledging its source.

Management by objectives was defined by John Humble (1972), a leading British enthusiast, as:

A dynamic system which seeks to integrate the company's need to clarify and achieve its profit and growth goals with the manager's need to contribute and develop himself (*sic*). It is a demanding and rewarding style of managing a business.

Management by objectives as described by John Humble

Management by objectives is a continuous process of:

- reviewing critically and restating the company's strategic and tactical plans;

- clarifying with each manager the key results and performance standards he must achieve, and gaining his contribution and commitment to these, individually and as a team member;

- agreeing with each manager a job improvement plan which makes a measurable and realistic contribution to the unit and company plans for better performance;

- providing conditions (an organization structure and management information) in which it is possible to achieve the key results and improvement plan;

- using systematic performance review to measure and discuss progress towards results;

- developing management training plans to build on strengths, to help managers to overcome their weaknesses and to get them to accept responsibility for self-development;

- strengthening the motivation of managers by effective selection, salary and succession plans.

Humble emphasized that these activities are interdependent and he illustrated the dynamic nature of the system, as shown in Figure 1.1. Except for the insistence that this system is exclusively for managers (who, presumably, were usually men) much of what Humble wrote would be acceptable today as good performance management practice. The performance management cycle as usually described today

Figure 1.1   The management by objectives cycle

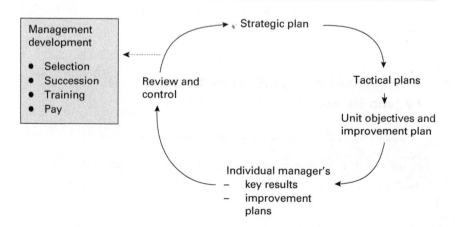

certainly derives from his management by objectives cycle, and the focus on objectives or goals is still a fundamental characteristic of performance management.

Management by objectives was adopted enthusiastically by many companies in the 1960s and '70s, but it became discredited by the 1990s – why? One of the first and most formidable attacks on management by objectives was made in the *Harvard Business Review* by Levinson (1976). His criticisms were:

- Every organization is a social system, a network of interpersonal relationships. A person doing an excellent job by objective standards of measurement may fail miserably as a partner, superior, subordinate or colleague.

- The greater the emphasis on measurement and quantification, the more likely the subtle, non-measurable elements of the task will be sacrificed. Quality of performance frequently loses out to quantification.

- It (management by objectives) leaves out the individual's personal needs and objectives, bearing in mind that the most powerful driving force for individuals comprises their needs, wishes and personal objectives.

These points apply equally to performance management practices today that focus on objectives.

The demise of management by objectives was mainly due to the fact that the process became over-systematized (often under the influence of package-oriented management consultants) and too much emphasis was placed on the quantification of objectives. The originators of the concept may not have advocated lots of forms and they recognized, as John Humble did, that qualitative performance standards could be included in the system, by which was meant 'a statement of conditions which exist when the result is being satisfactorily achieved'. But these principles were often ignored in practice. In addition, management by objectives often became a top-down affair with little dialogue, and it tended to focus narrowly on the objectives of individual managers without linking them to corporate or team goals (although this link was supposed to happen, and it was certainly a major part of Drucker's original concept). The system also tended to concentrate on managers, leaving the rest of the staff to be dealt with by an old-fashioned merit rating scheme, presumably because it was thought that they did not deserve anything better.

Developments in assessment techniques

Concurrently with the emergence of management by objectives, consideration was being given to avoiding the misguided use of traits in performance assessment. The critical incident approach developed by Flanagan (1954) changed the focus to the observation of behaviour. Behavioural anchored rating scales (Smith and Kendall, 1963) and behavioural observation scales (Latham and Wexley, 1977) provided for the quantification of behavioural performance.

Much research was carried out later on rating, for example, by Bernardin and Buckley (1981), Sulsky and Balzer (1988) and Murphy and Balzer (1989). Such activity reflected the preoccupation of some US academics with rating techniques. This still persists today. Rating research led to the emergence in the early 1990s of multi-source or 360-degree feedback, which provided for upwards and lateral assessments as well as the traditional top-down rating.

Results-oriented performance appraisal

In the 1970s a revised approach to performance assessment was developed under the influence of the management by objectives movement in that it incorporated the agreement of objectives and an assessment of the results obtained against these objectives. Ratings were usually retained of overall performance and in relation to individual objectives. Trait ratings were also used but, more recently, they were replaced in some schemes by competency ratings. This form of performance appraisal received a boost during the later 1980s because of the use of performance-related pay based on performance ratings.

However, many criticisms were made of the ways in which appraisal schemes operated in practice. Levinson (1976) wrote that: 'It is widely recognized that there are many things wrong with most of the performance appraisal systems in use.' He thought that the most obvious drawbacks were:

- Judgements on performance are usually subjective, impressionistic and arbitrary.
- Ratings by different managers are not comparable.
- Delays in feedback occur which create frustration when good performance is not quickly recognized and anger when judgement is rendered for inadequacies long past.
- Managers generally have a sense of inadequacy about appraising subordinates and paralysis and procrastination result from their feelings of guilt about playing God.

He stated that: 'Performance appraisal needs to be viewed not as a technique but as a process involving both people and data, and as such the whole process is inadequate.' He also pointed out that appraisal was not usually recognized as a normal function of management and that individual objectives were seldom related to the objectives of the business.

Another view was expressed by Long (1986) on the basis of the Institute of Personnel Management's research into performance appraisal:

> There is no such thing as the perfect performance review system. None is infallible, although some are more fallible than others. Some systems, despite flaws, will be managed fairly conscientiously; others, despite elegant design, will receive perfunctory attention and ultimately fail. The relative success or failure of performance review, as with any other organizational system, depends very much on the attitudinal response it arouses.

The requirements for success were indeed demanding. These were stated by Lazer and Wikstrom (1977) to be as follows:

> A 'good' performance appraisal scheme must be job related, reliable, valid for the purposes for which it is being used, standardized in its procedures, practical in its administration and suited to the organization's culture.

The problem was that performance appraisal was too often perceived as the property of the personnel department. This was where the forms were kept and where decisions were made about performance-related pay.

Line managers frequently criticized the system as being irrelevant. They felt they had better things to do and at worst ignored it and at best paid lip-service to completing the forms, knowing that they had to make ratings to generate performance pay. Indeed, managers have been known to rate first in accordance with what pay increase individuals should have and then write their comments to justify their marks. In other words, human beings behaved as human beings. Individuals were said to be wary of appraisals and as likely to be demotivated by an appraisal meeting as to be motivated.

Perhaps the worst feature of performance appraisal schemes was that appraisal was not regarded as a normal and necessary process of management. If ratings were based on a review of the extent to which individual objectives were attained, those objectives were not linked to the objectives of the business or department. Appraisal was isolated and therefore irrelevant. Managers tended to go through the motions when they reluctantly held their yearly appraisal meeting. As described by Armstrong and Murlis (1998) it too often became 'a dishonest annual ritual'.

The concept of 'Appraisal: an idea whose time has gone?' was advanced by Fletcher (1993) as follows.

Clive Fletcher on appraisal

What we are seeing is the demise of the traditional, monolithic appraisal system... In its place are evolving a number of separate but linked processes applied in different ways according to the needs of local circumstances and staff levels. The various elements in this may go by different names, and perhaps the term 'appraisal' has in some ways outlived its usefulness.

Enter performance management

The concept of performance management incorporates some of the notions and approaches of management by objectives and performance appraisal but it included a number of different features, as described opposite.

The earliest reference to performance management in the literature was made by Warren (1972). On the basis of his research in a manufacturing company he defined the features of performance management as follows. These requirements are just as apt today.

Features of performance management as defined by Malcolm Warren

1 *Expectations*: a large group of employees – preferably all – must be told clearly, objectively and in their own language what is specifically expected of them.

2 *Skill*: a large group of employees must have the technical knowledge and skill to carry out the tasks.

3 *Feedback*: workers must be told in clear terms, without threats, how they are doing in terms of expectations.

4 *Resources*: employees must have the time, money and equipment necessary to perform the expected tasks at optimal level.

5 *Reinforcement*: employees must be positively reinforced for desired performance.

Another early use of the term 'performance management' was made by Beer and Ruh (1976). Their thesis was that 'performance is best developed through practical challenges and experiences on the job with guidance and feedback from superiors'. They described the performance management system at Corning Glass Works, the aim of which was to help managers give feedback in a helpful and constructive way, and to aid in the creation of a developmental plan. The features of this system, which distinguished it from other appraisal schemes, were as follows:

● emphasis on both development and evaluation;

● use of a profile defining the individual's strengths and development needs;

● integration of the results achieved with the means by which they have been achieved;

● separation of development review from salary review.

Although this was not necessarily a model performance management process it did contain a number of characteristics that are still regarded as good practice.

The concept of performance management then lay fallow for some years but began to emerge in the United States as a new approach to managing performance in the mid-1980s. However, one of the first books exclusively devoted to performance management was not published until the late 1980s (Plachy and Plachy, 1988). They described what had by then become the accepted approach to performance management as follows.

Performance management as described by Plachy and Plachy

Performance management is communication: a manager and an employee arrive together at an understanding of what work is to be accomplished, how it will be accomplished, how work is progressing toward desired results, and finally, after effort is expended to accomplish the work, whether the performance has achieved the agreed-upon plan. The process recycles when the manager and employee begin planning what work is to be accomplished for the next performance period. Performance management is an umbrella term that includes performance *planning*, performance *review*, and performance *appraisal*. Major work plans and appraisals are generally made annually. Performance review occurs whenever a manager and an employee confirm, adjust, or correct their understanding of work performance during routine work contacts.

In the United Kingdom the first published reference to performance management was made at a meeting of the Compensation Forum in 1987 by Don Beattie, Personnel Director, ICL, who described how it was used as 'an essential contribution to a massive and urgent change programme in the organization' and had become a part of the fabric of the business.

By 1990 performance management had entered the vocabulary of human resource management in the United Kingdom as well as in the United States. In the United Kingdom Alan Fowler (1990) defined what has become the accepted concept of performance management:

Management has always been about getting things done, and good managers are concerned to get the right things done well. That, in essence, is performance management – the organization of work to achieve the best possible results. From this simple viewpoint, performance management is not a system or technique, *it is the totality of the day-to-day activities of all managers.* (Emphasis added.)

The following definition of performance management was produced as a result of the Institute of Personnel Management research:

A strategy which relates to every activity of the organization set in the context of its human resources policies, culture, style and communications systems. The nature of the strategy depends on the organizational context and can vary from organization to organization.

It was suggested that what was described as a 'performance management system' (PMS) complied with the textbook definition when the following characteristics were met by the organization.

Institute of Personnel Management (1992) definition of a performance management system

- It communicates a vision of its objectives to all its employees.
- It sets departmental and individual performance targets which are related to wider objectives.
- It conducts a formal review of progress towards these targets.
- It uses the review process to identify training, development and reward outcomes.
- It evaluates the whole process in order to improve effectiveness.
- It expresses performance targets in terms of measurable outputs, accountabilities and training/learning targets.
- It uses formal appraisal procedures as ways of communicating performance requirements which are set on a regular basis.
- It links performance requirements to pay, especially for senior managers.

With the exception of the link to pay, which applies to many but not all performance management schemes, these characteristics still hold good today. The IPM research established that in the organizations with performance management systems, 85 per cent had performance pay and 76 per cent rated performance (this proportion is lower in later surveys). The emphasis was on objective setting and review which, as the authors of the report mentioned, 'leaves something of a void when it comes to identifying development needs on a longer-term basis... there is a danger with results-orientated schemes in focusing excessively on *what* is to be achieved and ignoring the *how*'. It was noted that some organizations were moving in the direction of competency analysis but not very systematically.

Two of the IPM researchers (Bevan and Thompson, 1991) commented on the emergence of performance management systems as integrating processes that mesh various human resource management activities with the business objectives of the organization. They identified two broad thrusts towards integration: 1) *reward-driven integration*, which emphasizes the role of performance pay in changing organizational behaviour and tends to undervalue the part played by other human resource development (HRD) activities. This appeared to be the dominant mode of integration. 2) *Development-driven integration*, which stresses the importance of HRD. Although performance pay may operate in these organizations it is perceived to be complementary to HRD activities rather than dominating them. Some of the interesting conclusions emerging from this research are set out below.

Conclusions from the IPM (1992) research

- No evidence was found that improved performance in the private sector is associated with the presence of formal performance management programmes.

- An overwhelming body of psychological research exists which makes clear that, as a way of enhancing individual performance, the setting of performance targets is inevitably a successful strategy.

- The process of forming judgements and evaluations of individual performance is an almost continuous one. Most often it is a subconscious process, relying on subjective judgements, based on incomplete evidence and spiced with an element of bias.

- There was little consistency of viewpoint on the motivating power of money. The majority (of organizations) felt that the real motivators at management levels were professional and personal pride in the standards achieved, or loyalty to the organization and its aims, or peer pressure. One line manager commented that he was self-motivated: 'The money comes as a result of that, not as the cause of it.' While the principle of pay for performance was generally accepted, the reservations were about putting it into practice: 'It was often viewed as a good idea – especially for other people – but not something that, when implemented, seemed to breed either satisfaction or motivation.'

- The focus has been on the splendid-sounding notion of the performance-orientated culture and of improving the bottom line, and/or the delivery of services. Whilst this is well and good, the achievement of such ends has to be in concert with the aims and the development needs of individuals.

These conclusions are still relevant.

Performance management – the next phase

The 1998 IPD research project (Armstrong and Baron, 1998), revealed that in many instances performance management practices had moved on since 1992. In the organizations covered by the survey the following trends were observed:

- Performance management is regarded as a number of inter-linked processes.

- Performance management is seen as a continuous process, not as a once a year appraisal, thus echoing Fowler's (1990) comment that: 'In today's fast-moving world, any idea that effective performance management can be tied neatly to a single annual date is patently absurd'.

- A focus on employee development rather than on performance-related pay.
- A shift towards getting line managers to accept and own performance management as a natural process of management.
- A rejection in some organizations of the concept of a bureaucratic, centrally controlled and uniform system of performance management, and its replacement with the acceptance that, within an overall policy framework, different approaches may be appropriate in different parts of the organization and for different people.

Another important trend in the 1990s was the increased use of competencies for recruitment and people development purposes. This led to more focus on the nature of performance, which was recognized as being not only about what was achieved but also about *how* it was achieved. The result was the 'mixed model' of performance management, which covers competency levels and the extent to which behaviour is in line with the core values of the organization as well as objective setting and review.

The next development was the recognition that performance management had to focus on organizational as well as individual effectiveness. It was not enough to hope that processes for improving individual performance would necessarily result in improvements in organizational performance. A strategic approach was required that involves fitting the performance management strategy to the firm's business strategy and context and supporting the business and HR strategies through activities designed to improve organizational capability such as human capital management, talent management and the development of high performance cultures.

Features of performance management

Conceptually, performance management can be modelled in Figure 1.2 as a continuous cycle that corresponds with William Deming's (1986) plan-do-check-act model. But the reality of performance management as discussed in the next chapter is different.

Figure 1.2   The performance management cycle

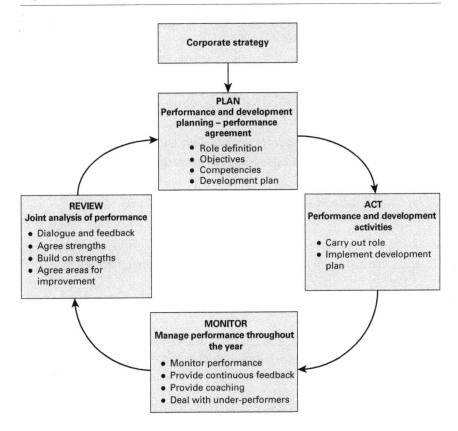

CASE STUDY   CEMEX UK

The following, which is an example of a typical performance management system, is operated by CEMEX UK, a supplier of cement, ready-mixed concrete and aggregates with 4,000 employees. It is a subsidiary of the Mexican company CEMEX.

Aims of performance management

The aims of the Performance and Potential Assessment (P&PA) scheme at CEMEX UK are to:

- promote strategic alignment and respond to business needs;
- facilitate clear communication and understanding of standards;

- ensure objective grading and differentiation of potential levels;
- promote continuous feedback and development;
- reinforce high performance attitudes.

The annual cycle

CEMEX's performance management scheme runs over the calendar year as follows:

- The company's overall budget is set in January and from this the most senior managers' objectives are established which are then cascaded down the organization.
- Around July, there is a mid-year review of initial objectives set and discussions on how the individual is progressing over the first part of the year.
- Finally, between November and January an ultimate meeting takes place where line managers and individuals meet and staff are rated between one and five by their line managers.

Objective setting

CEMEX states that the purpose of objectives is to communicate clearly the kind of work to be performed. The company says that there are three types of objectives that can be set:

1 Operative/functional: activities designed to strengthen the quality of service and to make the existing processes or procedures more efficient by innovation.

2 Continuous improvement: responsibilities that are inherent to the position and functional area of the employee.

3 Development and training: activities that will help the employee improve their performance.

Setting objectives is a two-way process and all objectives must align with the common acronym 'SMART'. Two more conditions are laid down – first, that objectives should be relevant, and second, that they should be limited in number (no more than 10 on the grounds that research has shown that any more than this amount limits impact and causes dilution.

Objectives are cascaded down through the organization, which promotes the alignment of objectives with the corporate strategy and ensures the level of challenge among the overall team is calibrated. In practice, direct supervisors can cascade objectives down by up to two levels, while indirect supervisors can do so by one level.

In addition, the various objectives are weighted and each has a specific unit of measure. For example, a sales person might have a specific amount of a product to sell which means that there is no ambiguity and it is easy to determine whether this sort of target has been achieved or not.. By using clear evaluation criteria with a description of what it means to accomplish them, CEMEX believes that there can be no disagreement when it comes to determining a score for the year.

Mid-year and final review

CEMEX recognizes that the individual's and company's situation can change over the course of the year so a further mid-year review is held in July. This ensures that managers can amend objectives as a consequence of any work or other changes that have taken place. The end-of-year meeting takes place between November and January when there is a one-to-one discussion between the employee and his or her immediate supervisor. At the meeting, a final rating is agreed that helps determine the bonus to be received the following March.

360-degree appraisal

CEMEX's performance management scheme also incorporates a 360-degree appraisal process whereby managers, staff and clients provide additional feed-back. Although the results of this are considered when determining bonus levels, this process is designed mainly to gauge the future potential of the individual with the main rating more important in the bonus decision.

The 360-degree appraisal does consider outcomes, but perhaps more impor-tant is an emphasis on 'how' people accomplish their objectives, drawing on the company's nine key competencies:

1 Team work: genuine willingness to work with others in a cooperative, assertive and transparent manner to achieve a common goal, placing group interests above those of the individual.

2 Creativity: generation and development of ideas, considering both internal and external context to create and take advantage of business opportunities in CEMEX.

3 Focus on stakeholders: adaptation of personal behaviour to the values, priorities and objectives of CEMEX, looking for the benefit of the different stakeholders.

4 Entrepreneurial spirit: development of opportunities to improve the business, within and outside one's own working environment, undertaking risks and over-coming obstacles.

5 Strategic thinking: understanding the circumstances that prevail in the external environment and those within the company, to make decisions that lead to the achievement of CEMEX's strategies.

6 Customer service orientation: willingness to serve and anticipate the needs of the client, both internal and external, and to take the necessary actions to satisfy them.

7 Development of others: continuous commitment to stimulate learning and development of others, in order to further their professional success.

8 Information management: ability to search, generate, manage and share relevant information for decision making in the organization.

9 Development of alliances: identify and maintain long-term relationships with individuals, groups and institutions, both within and outside the organization, which contribute to the achievement of CEMEX's strategies.

The 360-degree process allows up to six people to appraise each staff member. These include any individuals that have observed their behaviours in relationship to the competencies and should include at least one internal client, at least one internal supplier and at least one peer. Once the individuals have selected their evaluators, the immediate manager either approves or rejects those chosen. This may even involve the rejection of the entire proposal, in which case the employee will need to come up with a new set of evaluators. When examining a proposal, line managers are advised to avoid approving the same evaluators over a number of years in order to promote greater diversity.

Online tool

CEMEX's online tool, known as CEMEX Plaza, enables managers and staff to enter and store all of the information and results produced from the 360-degree appraisals.

Bonus scheme

Bonuses are determined by an individual's rating in the end-of-year appraisal meeting, as long as threshold financial performance has been achieved by his or her own unit, in the UK. In some cases, for more senior staff, the performance of CEMEX Worldwide can also be a factor. Objectives are graded on a five-point scale, with a corresponding numerical value:

Significantly above target = 5

Above target = 4

On target = 3

Below target = 2

Unsatisfactory = 1

The final rating is the weighted average of the different objectives.

Non-performers

Anyone who receives a score of 2 or below at the end-of-year meeting is considered to be performing below the level that CEMEX expects and in such cases action is taken. The initial step in the process is to set up a specific programme to help the employee improve. If this is not successful a 'safety track' is put in place with 'mini objectives' that are shorter-term than the annual ones. Where necessary the line manager, along with the HR department, engages in training and development and coaching to help the employee improve his or her performance.

Conclusions

The overarching principles governing effective performance management were defined as follows by Egan (1995):

> Most employees want direction, freedom to get their work done, and encouragement not control. The performance management system should be a control system only by exception. The solution is to make it a collaborative development system in two ways. First, the entire performance management process – coaching, counselling, feedback, tracking, recognition, and so forth – should encourage development. Ideally, team members grow and develop through these interactions. Second, when managers and team members ask what they need to be able to do to do bigger and better things, they move to strategic development.

This is an ideal concept of performance management It is achievable using the approaches described above; but in the opinion of many commentators and the evidence from the research described in the next chapter, only with considerable difficulty. Performance management is many-faceted and demands great skills from everyone involved. This feature was commented on by Cascio (2010): 'It is an exercise in observation and judgement, it is a feedback process, it is an organizational intervention. It is a measurement process as well as an intensely emotional process. Above all, it is an inexact, human process.'

References

Armstrong, M and Baron, A (1998) *Performance Management: The new realities*, CIPD, London

Armstrong, M and Baron, A (2005) *Managing Performance: Performance management in action*, CIPD, London

Armstrong, M and Murlis, H (1998) *Reward Management*, 4th edn, Kogan Page, London

Beer, M and Ruh, R A (1976) Employee growth through performance management, *Harvard Business Review*, July–August, pp 59–66

Bernardin, H J and Buckley, M R (1981) Strategies in rater training, *Academy of Management Review*, 6, pp 205–12

Bevan, S and Thompson, M (1991) Performance management at the cross-roads, *Personnel Management*, November, pp 36–39

Cascio, W F (2010) *Managing Human Resources: Productivity, quality of work life, profits*, 8th edn, McGraw-Hill Irwin, New York

Deming, W E (1986) *Out of the Crisis*, Massachusetts Institute of Technology Centre for Advanced Engineering Studies, Cambridge, MA

Drucker, P (1955) *The Practice of Management*, Heinemann, London

Egan, G (1995) A clear path to peak performance, *People Management*, 18 May, pp 34–37

e-reward (2004) *Performance Management Survey*, e-reward, Stockport

Flanagan, J C (1954) The critical incident technique, *Psychological Bulletin*, 51, pp 327–58

Fletcher, C (1993) Appraisal: an idea whose time has gone? *Personnel Management*, September, pp 34–37

Fowler, A (1990) Performance management: the MBO of the '90s? *Personnel Management*, July, pp 47–54

Humble, J (1972) *Management by Objectives*, Management Publications, London

Institute of Personnel Management (1992) *Performance Management in the UK: An analysis of the issues*, IPM, London

Koontz, H (1971) *Appraising Managers as Managers*, McGraw-Hill, New York

Latham, G P and Wexley, K N (1977) Behavioural observation scales, *Personnel Psychology*, **30**, pp 255–68

Lazer, R I and Wikstrom, W S (1977) *Appraising Managerial Performance: Current practices and new directions*, The Conference Board, New York

Levinson, H (1976) Appraisal of *what* performance? *Harvard Business Review*, July–August, pp 30–46

Long, P (1986) *Performance Appraisal Revisited*, Institute of Personnel Management, London

McGregor, D (1957) An uneasy look at performance appraisal, *Harvard Business Review*, May–June, pp 89–94

McGregor, D (1960) *The Human Side of Enterprise*, McGraw-Hill, New York

Murphy, K R and Balzer, W K (1989) Rater errors and rating accuracy, *Journal of Applied Psychology*, **74** (4), pp 619–24

Plachy, R J and Plachy, S J (1988) *Getting Results from Your Performance Management and Appraisal System*, AMACOM, New York

Rowe, K (1964) An appraisal of appraisals, *Journal of Management Studies*, **1** (1), pp 1–25

Smith, P C and Kendall, L M (1963) Retranslation of expectations: an approach to the construction of unambiguous answers for rating scales, *Journal of Applied Psychology*, **47**, pp 853–85

Sulsky, L M and Balzer, W K (1988) The meaning and measurement of performance rating accuracy: Some methodological and theoretical concerns, *Journal of Applied Psychology*, **73**, pp 497–506

Taylor, F W (1911) *Principles of Scientific Management*, Harper, New York

Warren, M (1972) Performance management: a substitute for supervision, *Management Review*, October, pp 28–42

Performance management – the reality

02

Performance management, as described in the previous chapter, is a systematic and continuous process for improving organizational performance by developing the performance of individuals and teams. However, it promises much but delivers little, and this chapter explains why this is the case. It is divided into three parts: a selection of the many criticisms levelled at performance management over the years, a summary of the research on how performance management is working, and an explanation of why it fails.

Performance management in the dock

The following accusations are about the inadequacies of performance appraisal and performance management (the former term is often taken to be synonymous with performance management but properly only refers to its elements of review, assessment and rating).

Keith Grint (1993), now Professor of Public Leadership & Management at Warwick Business School, asserted, famously, that: 'Rarely in the history of business can such a system (performance management) have promised so much and delivered so little.' John Shields (2007) argued that: 'Ill-chosen, badly designed or poorly implemented performance management schemes can communicate entirely the wrong messages as to what the organization expects from its employees.'

W Edwards Deming, the quality guru, claimed in his diatribe *The Annual Appraisal: Destroyer of people* (1987) that:

> The performance appraisal nourishes short-term performance, annihilates long-term planning, builds fear, demolishes teamwork, nourishes rivalry and politics... it leaves people bitter, crushed, bruised, battered, desolate, despondent, dejected, feeling inferior, some even depressed, unfit for work for weeks after receipt of rating, unable to comprehend why they are inferior. It is unfair, as it ascribes to the people in a group differences that may be caused totally by the system that they work in.

This may be a trifle hard on performance appraisal – it can be quite bad, but is it as bad as all that? Some years later Tom Coens and Mary Jenkins (2002) delivered the following judgement:

> Throughout our work lives, most of us have struggled with performance appraisal. No matter how many times we redesign it, retrain the supervisors, or give it a new name, it never comes out right. Again and again, we see supervisors procrastinate or just go through the motions, with little taken to heart. And the supervisors who do take it to heart and give it their best mostly meet disappointment.

Duncan Brown, Head of HR Consultancy at the Institute for Employment Studies, observed that:

> The problems [of performance management] are... not of ambition or intent, but rather practice and delivery. Low rates of coverage and even more frequently low quality conversations and non-existent follow-up are commonplace, in the wake of uncommitted directors, incompetent line managers, uncomprehending employees and hectoring HR with their still complex and bureaucratic HR processes.
>
> (Brown, 2010)

Performance management issues in the United Kingdom, as listed by Professor Paul Sparrow, Director of the Centre for Performance-led HR at Lancaster University, include:

- the ability to produce higher levels of employee engagement as opposed to just more self-awareness or measurement accuracy;
- the level of alignment between rewards (in their fullest sense) produced by the performance management system, and the varied

needs of diverse employee segments, who may be working to very different psychological contracts;

- the extent to which stand-alone performance management systems contribute directly to value creation in the organization or rather serve more to protect value by managing only marginal risks. (Sparrow, 2008)

According to Pulakos *et al* (2008) the main problems with performance management in the United States are as follows:

- Performance management is regarded as an administrative burden to be minimized rather than an effective strategy to obtain business results.
- Managers and employees are reluctant to engage in candid performance discussions.
- Judgement and time factors impede accurate performance assessments.

How well is performance management working? Lessons from research

A considerable amount of research has been carried out on performance management, most of it with negative results. Summaries of a number of studies are set out below.

Guest and Conway (1998)

An analysis by Guest and Conway covered the 388 organizations with performance management surveyed by Armstrong and Baron (2005). The key criteria used for determining the effectiveness of performance management were the achievement of financial targets, development of skills, development of competence, improved customer care and improved quality. Against these criteria, over 90 per cent of respondents rated performance management as being moderately or highly effective.

However, there were caveats. The analysis indicated that the opinions of respondents to the survey should all be viewed with extreme caution since they are often based on a very limited form of formal evaluation, or on an absence of any formal evaluation. This raises serious questions about the basis for the generally positive assessment of performance management.

Further, more detailed statistical analysis of the replies to the questionnaire failed to demonstrate consistent evidence of any link between the practice of performance management and outcomes such as the achievement of financial targets, of quality and customer service goals and employee development goals. The conclusion reached was that this survey has not shown that performance management has an impact on overall organizational performance.

McDonald and Smith (1991)

The findings of this study contrasted with the outcome of a survey by McDonald and Smith covering 437 publicly quoted US companies. They established that the 205 respondents that had performance management, as opposed to those without, had:

- higher profits, better cash flows, stronger stock market performance and higher stock value;
- significant gains over three years in financial performance and productivity;
- higher sales growth per employee;
- lower real growth in number of employees.

The researchers commented that: 'In the successful companies the difference in managing employee performance seems to be that it is regarded as a mainstream business issue, not an isolated "personnel problem".'

This is not as convincing as it looks. It is in fact a classic case of reversed causality (a situation where A might have caused B but it is just as likely that B caused A). Performance management systems may have generated successful companies but it could equally be the case that the successful companies were the ones with the inclination and money to introduce sophisticated practices such as performance management.

Corporate Leadership Council (2002)

The following comments about the importance and difficulty of improving employee performance were made by some of the 19,000 respondents to a survey:

> 'A system that drives improvements in employee performance drives improvements in your business. If you can't use reviews to improve employee performance, then what's the point?' *VP of HR, European manufacturer*

> 'The manager has a critical role in driving high employee performance, and HR needs to provide managers with the support to do that well. The problem is we don't really know which manager behaviours drive good employee performance.' *VP of HR, North American healthcare company*

> 'There are many drivers of high performance – leadership, recognition, development. But it is extremely difficult to figure out how to actually create a high-performance environment.' *VP of HR, South African financial services firm*

> 'We've learnt that you have to have the right reward structure in place or your performance management system won't work. But beyond aligning performance criteria and rewards, we struggle with knowing what else we can do to make sure we're getting the best performance from our employees.' *VP of HR, European retailer*

McAdam, Hazlett and Casey (2005)

Research in a public sector organization indicated that staff at all levels understood the new performance management system and perceived it as being beneficial. However, there were concerns that the approach was not continuously managed throughout the year and was in danger of becoming an annual event rather than an on-going process. Furthermore, the change process seemed to have advanced without corresponding changes to appraisal and reward and recognition systems. Thus, the business objectives were not aligned with motivating factors within the organization. It was argued that there is a need for increased understanding in relation to developing appropriate performance management approaches within the context of the public sector, particularly the complexity of multiple stakeholders and difficulties in simply adapting and transferring private sector solutions.

Armstrong and Ward (2005)

This research was based on six detailed case studies. It was concluded that the variety of approaches taken by the case study organizations showed that when it comes to performance management, one size does not fit all. Organizations need to be clear about the purpose of performance management. The challenge is for it to retain a strategic role rather than tending towards tactical activities, such as the process. It was suggested by the researchers that:

1 Performance management is not a single intervention that can be implemented easily. It relies on a range of activities, involving several core HR processes, and requires these to be carefully integrated.

2 A sophisticated 'process' does not always lead to effective performance management.

3 It is difficult to improve management capability in managing performance.

4 There is an enduring underlying belief that performance management is a good thing to do. However, there is a reluctance in organizations to evaluate the effectiveness of performance management systems and to harness the results of research.

5 There is often a lack of understanding about the nature of the link between performance and organizational culture, and the implications for performance management. Performance management reflects the organizational culture and context.

6 When the performance management system is not delivering, it is likely to be reflecting a deeper issue such as lack of organizational

agreement about clarity of purpose, priorities or standards, or a mismatch between espoused values and actual behaviours.

7 Aligning the performance management process with the direction of any desired organizational change is essential.

8 It can support organizational change but may not be the only or main driver of it.

Chartered Institute of Personnel and Development (2009)

A total of 507 individuals responded to a web-based survey. In reply to the question of what performance management could achieve, the highest level of agreement (30 per cent) was to the assertion that performance management enables individuals to understand what they ought to be doing; 13 per cent disagreed and 57 per cent neither agreed nor disagreed. Twenty-three per cent agreed that performance management helped line managers to manage people better, but 25 per cent disagreed. Only 20 per cent agreed that performance management had a positive impact on individual performance, and 21 per cent disagreed.

The comment was made that: 'Over the years the evidence has tended to suggest that the process of performance management is less important than its positioning, implementation and objectives' (CIPD, 2009: 4).

WorldatWork and Sibson (2010)

A survey established that the top three performance management challenges reported by respondents were: 1) managers lack courage to have difficult performance discussions (63 per cent); 2) performance management is viewed as an 'HR process' instead of as a 'business critical process' (47 per cent); and 3) that they experienced poor goal setting (36 per cent). They also noted that: 'Too much attention has been placed on the design of a [performance management] system and not enough on how it works when implemented.'

Institute for Employment Studies (Hirsh et al, 2011)

The conclusion reached by the research was that:

> Managers and employees in the IES study not only found the PM [performance management] process complex and bureaucratic. They felt this completely masked its fundamental purpose. The commonest criticism by both managers and employees was that it was a box-ticking or form-filling exercise... The loudest message from HR and senior managers is of the need to get the forms filled in on time – a message about administrative compliance. So again in a real sense HR is asking for form-filling, so should not be surprised when managers say it feels like form-filling!

Here are some of the comments made by managers and employees who took part in this study:

> 'Performance management is seen as something you do to keep HR quiet. It's seen as owned by HR, not about how you manage people properly.'

> 'Managers don't give honest feedback and employees don't tell managers what they are thinking. There is no real conversation. 360-degree feedback is sought only from those who will say positive things.'

> 'There is no action resulting from the performance review.'

Duncan Brown (2011) observed on the basis of this research that:

> The main areas of concern [about performance management] were the skills and attitudes of reviewing managers, the consistency and quality of approach across large organizations, the complexity of the paperwork and the value of outputs... Performance management, it appears, isn't working.

Society of Human Resource Management (2012)

The conclusions reached by this SHRM study were that:

> Traditional performance management processes are often perceived as burdensome, demotivating and without value... Despite years

of research and practice, dissatisfaction with performance management (PM) is at an all-time high. More than 75 per cent of managers,
employees and heads of HR feel that PM results are ineffective and/or
inaccurate. Additionally, study after study has shown that the performance review is dreaded – it is not only perceived to be of little value
but it is highly demotivating to employees, even the highest performers.
Between formal goal-setting processes, mid-year and year-end reviews,
and often extensive rating and calibration processes, a great deal of time
and effort is expended on PM activities, costing organizations millions
annually with questionable returns.

Towers Watson (2012)

The three conclusions from this survey, with 384 participants across
Europe, were that:

1 Only just over a third (36 per cent) of employers say that performance management programmes are effective.
2 Forty-seven per cent of organizations have already introduced or
plan to introduce new technology to enable better processes.
3 Over half of companies say that managers lack the necessary skills
and time to manage performance really well.

It was commented that:

It is not surprising when employers, managers and employees all
say they are dissatisfied with performance management. Despite
headline-grabbing accounts of companies going rating-less, only a
small number of organizations have actually abandoned performance
management programmes or eliminated ratings altogether.

Chartered Institute of Personnel and Development (2014)

A survey of employees' views in 2014 on the fairness of performance
management processes found that less than half (46 per cent) believed
that they are very or somewhat fair, while a fifth believed that they
are somewhat or very unfair.

Conclusions

The chorus of disapproval is almost universal. There has been only one fairly recent study that has produced favourable results. This was a survey by Houldsworth and Jirasinghe (2006) of the opinions of line managers about performance management, which established that 68 per cent of respondents believed that it was very effective or excellent in their organization. All the other studies have found fault in design (eg too complex), or in execution (mainly with performance appraisal or review problems and the role of HR and line managers). The reasons for the failure of performance management are discussed below.

Why does performance management fail?

If you ask HR people why performance management fails they often say that it is all the fault of line managers who are uncommitted to doing it, doing it badly, or both. The e-reward (2014) survey of performance management revealed that the three major concerns of the HR respondents were:

1 The lack of line managers with the skills required to carry out performance management effectively.

2 Line managers who are reluctant to conduct performance management reviews.

3 Line managers who do not discriminate sufficiently when assessing performance.

However, if you ask line managers the same question they are likely to say that it is the fault of HR who impose a complex and unworkable system on them, police their efforts but fail to give adequate support, and have unrealistic expectations about what *their* performance management system can achieve because they do not really understand what is involved in managing performance.

The line managers are right. The blame for the failure of performance management generally rests with HR. It is HR people and the HR consultants who advise them who design over-complex systems.

For example, in a not-for-profit organization the appraisal forms to be filled in by line managers are six pages long. It is HR people who insist on an annual performance review that demands a level of skill few managers can reasonably be expected to attain and is in any case dreaded by all concerned. It is HR people who insist on ratings and demonstrate their lack of trust in line managers by adopting forced distribution systems (compelling managers to conform to a laid down distribution of performance ratings). It is HR people who fail to persuade management that there has to be a substantial investment in training to ensure that managers acquire essential basic skills in performance management activities such as providing feedback, agreeing goals, preparing development plans and dealing with under-performers. It is HR people who spend their time policing the efforts of line managers rather than supporting them. It is HR people who lack the understanding of business needed to advise on the development of a high performance culture – an essential ingredient for the success of performance management. It is HR people who fail to get sustained backing from top management, also essential to performance management's success. The main issues are discussed in more detail below.

Complexity

Complexity can arise from the design of performance management documentation but, more important, it is inherent in the process as usually applied. Appraisals are often expected to fulfil numerous functions including performance improvement, feedback, coaching, goal setting, skill development, the identification of potential, pay determination and the identification of under-performers. No performance appraisal system can meet all these ends. Peter Reilly (2015) commented that:

> All-singing, all-dancing performance appraisal... requires managers
> to review a wide range of content (reward, training needs, business
> alignment, etc) and use of multiple processes (personal development
> planning, performance ranking, potential assessment, etc), but also to
> apply different modes of management – appreciation, evaluation and
> coaching – which can be very tough on them to deliver.

It is no wonder that line managers do not live up to the expectations of HR or that the perfunctory training in performance management provided by most organizations fails to produce the multi-skilled, multi-tasking paragon the system demands.

Lack of a high performance culture

Managing performance is what managers do. They will do it best if the organization has a pervading and powerful high performance culture, one in which its values, norms and practices combine to create a climate in which the achievement of high levels of performance is a way of life. In such a culture, management is absolutely clear about the levels of performance to be achieved and how they should be achieved, and conveys its expectations to all employees. Without such a culture performance management systems wither on the vine.

Lack of leadership from the top

Performance management cannot thrive without leadership from top management. The CEO, supported by the top team, should take the initiative, set the direction and maintain the tone. The creation of a high performance culture is very much his or her responsibility. Leaving it all to HR is a recipe for failure. When members of the top management team do not lead by example, demonstrate their belief in performance management and continually impress on all concerned the importance of managing performance in accordance with the organization's guidelines, line managers will lose interest. They will dismiss the performance management system as an imposition from HR and only go through the motions, if at all.

Poor design

It was observed by Lee (2005) that:

> Most traditional performance appraisal schemes are fundamentally flawed as they are counterproductive by design. The stated purpose of these systems is to measure and rate past performance when, in reality,

the goal of any performance management system should be performance enhancement... No one has the power to alter the past, so it is far wiser to direct attention and efforts to the future.

This highlights two basic performance management design issues: 1) *The extent to which the system should be forward-looking.* A forward-looking approach is fundamental to the concept of performance management. Although past performance will be analysed, the only reason for doing this is to identify any areas where future performance can be enhanced and how this should be done. 2) *The extent to which the system should focus on performance enhancement.* As indicated above, this should be the main purpose of performance management. It does not exist simply to inform performance pay decisions or to identify under-performing people.

The process of design too often focuses on the development of an ideal system without giving sufficient consideration to how it will be implemented. The result may be unrealistic expectations about what managers will be able or willing to do. This problem will be compounded by failures to involve managers sufficiently in the design process.

Poor implementation

An inadequate approach to implementation is often a major cause of failure. It is not too difficult to conceptualize how performance management should function; it is much harder to ensure that it works in practice. It takes time, energy and determination to launch performance management successfully and to ensure that it continues to operate effectively. This does not happen when insufficient attention is given to communicating why performance management is important, how everyone involved can benefit from it and how it should work. Neither will it happen if management training is undertaken on a 'sheep dip' basis – subjecting everyone to a half-day programme of instruction and exhortation that cannot possibly develop the skills and commitment required. Individual coaching and mentoring are often rejected because they are time-consuming and costly. A further reason for implementation failure is neglecting the training of staff at the receiving end. Performance management works best when it is treated as a partnership between managers and individual members of their teams. The latter also need to understand the part they are expected to play and how they should play it. The process of introducing performance management must concentrate on ensuring that worthy ambitions are translated into effective action by all concerned.

It is notable that most organizations that took part in the survey of performance management (e-reward, 2014) are at least considering ways in which they can alter and improve their performance management systems, with over half of those surveyed saying that they have made changes to their arrangements in the last five years.

Lessons from neuroscience

Research by the Neuro-Leadership Institute reported by David Rock and colleagues (Rock *et al*, 2014) showed why numbers-based performance management is obsolete. Labelling people with any form of numerical rating or ranking automatically generates an overwhelming 'fight or flight' response that impairs good judgement. This neural response is the same type of 'brain hijack' that occurs when there is an imminent physical threat like a confrontation with a wild animal. It primes people for rapid reaction and aggressive movement; it is ill-suited for the kind of thoughtful, reflective conversation that allows people to learn from a performance review. A neuroscience-based framework devised by David Rock (2009) indicates that five organizational factors have an immense, but often unnoticed, effect on negative human reactions. These factors are *status* (the perception of being considered better or worse than others); *certainty* (the predictability of future events); *autonomy* (the level of control people feel over their lives); *relatedness* (the experience of sharing goals with others); and *fairness* (the sense of being respected and treated equitably, especially compared with others). When an organization's perceived level of any of these factors is low, people feel threatened and perturbed.

Another problem with performance management identified by neuroscience is that it fosters an incorrect but prevalent view of human growth and learning. Carol Dweck (2006), Professor of

Psychology at Stanford University, has discovered that most people hold one of two implicit theories about human growth and learning. The 'fixed mind-set', as she calls it, holds that intelligence and talent are basically established at birth and remain static throughout life. People are born smart or not, and there's not much anyone can do about it. The 'growth mind-set', by contrast, holds that people learn, grow and improve all their lives. However, they could learn far more effectively, and bring more of a high performance attitude to everything they did, if they weren't held back by the mental paralysis associated with the fixed mind-set. The fixed mind-set is often reinforced by performance management systems, and when this happens people will typically strive to avoid difficult challenges. Any demanding objective will be seen as an invitation to fail. When reinventing performance management it is necessary to encourage managers to adopt a growth mind-set and thus promote continuous development.

Conclusions

The evidence suggests that performance management is too often an expensive, complex system for making people unhappy. It can fail when expectations are much higher than the ability to deliver results. Any of the factors listed above will create problems with performance management, but they can combine in various ways leading to total failure. So a badly designed and complex system can be poorly implemented in an environment where high performance is not given sufficient priority and where the onus of delivering performance management is left to HR rather than being the concern of top management.

References

Armstrong, K and Ward, A (2005) *What Makes for Effective Performance Management?* The Work Foundation, London

Armstrong, M and Baron, A (2005) *Managing Performance: Performance management in action*, CIPD, London

Brown, D (2010) Practice what we preach? Posted by Reward Blogger, 6 December, CIPD, London

Brown, D (2011) Performance management – can it ever work? *Manager,* Summer, p 16

CIPD (2009) *Performance Management in Action: Current trends and practices,* CIPD, London

CIPD (2014) *Employee Outlook,* http://www.cipd.co.uk/hr-resources/ survey-reports/employee-outlook-autumn-2014.aspx (accessed 16 November 2015)

Coens, T and Jenkins, M (2002) *Abolishing Performance Appraisals: Why they backfire and what to do instead,* Berrett-Koehler, San Francisco, CA

Corporate Leadership Council (2002) http://talentexperiment.com/images/ CLC_Building_the_High_Performance_Workforce_A_Quantitative_ Analysis_of_the_Effectiveness_of_Performance_Management_ Strategies_1_pdf (accessed 20 January 2016)

Deming, W E (1987) *The Annual Appraisal: Destroyer of people,* quoted by Ossini, J M (2013) *The Essential Deming,* The W Edwards Deming Institute, Ketchum, ID

Dweck, C S (2006) *Mindset: The new psychology of success,* Random House, New York

e-reward (2014) *Survey of Performance Management Practice,* e-reward, Stockport

Grint, K (1993) What's wrong with performance appraisal? A critique and a suggestion, *Human Resource Management Journal,* **3** (3) pp 61–77

Guest, D E and Conway, N (1998) An analysis of the results of the IPD performance management survey, in (eds) M Armstrong and A Baron, *Performance Management: The new realities,* IPD, London

Hirsh, W, Brown, D, Chubb, C and Reilly, P (2011) *Performance Management: The implementation challenge,* Institute for Employment Studies, http://www.employment-studies.co.uk/system/files/resources/ files/mp89.pdf) (accessed 10 March 2016)

Houldsworth, E and Jirasinghe, D (2006) *Managing and Measuring Employee Performance,* Kogan Page, London

Lee, C D (2005) Rethinking the goals of your performance management system, *Employment Relations Today,* **32** (3), pp 53–60

McAdam, R, Hazlett, S-A and Casey, C (2005) Performance management in the UK public sector: addressing multiple stakeholder complexity, *International Journal of Public Sector Management,* **18** (3), pp 256–73

McDonald, D and Smith, A (1991) A proven connection: performance management and business results, *Compensation & Benefits Review*, January–February, pp 59–64

Pulakos, E D, Mueller-Hanson, R A and O'Leary, R S (2008) Performance management in the US, in (eds) A Varma, P S Budhwar and A DeNisi, *Performance Management Systems: A global perspective*, Routledge, Abingdon

Reilly, P (2015) *Performance Management: Improving the delivery/improving the performance in practice*, IES, Brighton

Rock, D (2009) *Managing with the Brain in Mind*, Strategy+Business, New York

Rock, D, Davis, J and Jones, B (2014) *Kill Your Performance Ratings*, Strategy+Business, http://www.strategy-business.com/article/00275?gko=c442b (accessed 16 January 2016)

Shields, J (2007) *Managing Employee Performance and Reward*, Cambridge University Press, Port Melbourne

Society of Human Resource Management (2012) Performance Management Survey, http://www.shrm.org/HRStandards/PublishedStandards/Pages/ANSISHRM090012012,%20Performance%20Management.aspx (accessed 22 December 2015)

Sparrow, P (2008) Performance management in the UK, in (eds) A Varma, P S Budhwar and A DeNisi, *Performance Management Systems: A global perspective*, Routledge, Abingdon

Towers Watson (2012) *Global Workforce Study*, Towers Watson, London, https://www.towerswatson.com/en-GB/Insights/IC-Types/Survey-Research-Results/2015/12/Traditional-approaches-to-performance-management-still-dominant (accessed 16 January 2016)

WorldatWork and Sibson (2010) *The State of Performance Management*, WorldatWork, Scottsdale, AZ

Effective performance management

03

This chapter is about what can be done in general to improve performance management. It refers to *effective practice* in performance management, not *best practice*. There is no such thing as 'best practice performance management': what is best depends on the circumstances, especially the culture of the organization. There are no universal precepts, only guidelines produced by researchers and practitioners. Pulakos *et al* (2008) summed this up as follows:

> Performance management is often referred to as the 'Achilles heel' of HRM. All modern organizations face the challenge of how best to manage performance. That is, they must determine the best ways to set goals, evaluate work and distribute rewards in such a way that performance can be improved over time. While all firms face similar challenges, the way a firm responds to these challenges will depend on where the firm is located and the context within which it is operating. Differences in culture, technology or simply tradition make it difficult to directly apply techniques that have worked in one setting to a different setting.

Guidelines on effective practice in performance management

Over the years an immense amount of advice has been given on how performance management should be operated. A number of the most helpful suggestions are summarized in the following pages.

Principles of performance management

The overarching principles governing effective performance management were defined as follows by Egan (1995):

> Most employees want direction, freedom to get their work done, and encouragement not control. The performance management system should be a control system only by exception. The solution is to make it a collaborative development system, in two ways. First, the entire performance management process – coaching, counselling, feedback, tracking, recognition, and so forth – should encourage development. Ideally, team members grow and develop through these interactions. Second, when managers and team members ask what they need to be able to do to do bigger and better things, they move to strategic development.

Strebler *et al* (2001) suggested that the principles set out below were required for performance management to work effectively:

1 Have clear aims and measurable success criteria.

2 Be designed and implemented with appropriate employee involvement.

3 Be simple to understand and operate.

4 Have its effective use core to all management goals.

5 Allow employees a clear 'line of sight' between their performance goals and those of the organization.

6 Focus on role clarity and performance improvement.

7 Be closely allied to a clear and adequately resourced training and development infrastructure.

8 Make crystal clear the purpose of any direct link to reward and build in proper equity and transparency safeguards.

9 Be regularly and openly reviewed against its success criteria.

The views of practitioners on the principles of performance management as identified in the research conducted by Armstrong and Baron (1998; 2005) were as follows:

'Performance management is what managers do: a natural process of management.'

'A management tool which helps managers to manage.'

'It's about how we manage people – it's not a system.'

'Driven by corporate purpose and values.'

'To obtain solutions that work.'

'Only interested in things you can do something about and get a visible improvement.'

'Focus on changing behaviour rather than paperwork.'

'Based on accepted principles but operates flexibly.'

'Focus on development not pay.'

'Success depends on what the organization is and needs to be in its performance culture.'

Two further important principles were suggested by Sparrow and Hiltrop (1994): first, that top management must support and be committed to the system; and second, that it should be owned and driven by line management. It is evident that managers down the line will only take performance management seriously if it is clear to them that top managers believe in it and act accordingly. Also, performance management will only work if line managers want it to work and are capable of doing so. Both these principles emphasize that the bad old days of performance appraisal as the property of the personnel or HR department should be ended.

Ethical principles

Performance management should also operate in accordance with agreed and understood ethical principles. These have been defined by Winstanley and Stuart-Smith (1996) as:

1 *Respect for the individual* – people should be treated as 'ends in themselves' and not merely as 'means to other ends'.

2 *Mutual respect* – the parties involved in performance management should respect each other's needs and preoccupations.

3 *Procedural fairness* – the procedures incorporated in performance management should be operated fairly in accordance with the principles of procedural justice.

4 *Transparency* – people affected by decisions emerging from performance management processes should have an opportunity to scrutinize the basis upon which decisions were made.

Procedural justice requires that performance management decisions are made in accordance with principles that safeguard fairness, accuracy, consistency, transparency and freedom from bias, and properly consider the views and needs of employees. Folger *et al* (1992) set out the benefits of procedurally just performance management based on the components of due process. They labelled such systems 'due process performance management' and argued that they do not bring about gross reallocations of power between managers and employees, but rather require only that managers be open to employees' input and responsive to justifiable questions and concerns about performance standards and judgements.

Organizational researchers such as Taylor *et al* (1995) have gathered a strong body of evidence showing that employees care a great deal about the justice of performance management practices. This work generally has found that the more just or fair employees consider such systems to be, the more satisfied and accepting they are of the resultant outcomes, even when those outcomes are less than desirable. They found that procedurally just performance systems may also increase managers' own positive outcomes. The strength of these findings has led some researchers such as Folger and Cropanzano (1998) to propose that the provision of fair procedures is a more powerful foundation for the management of employees than is the provision of financial rewards.

Building a high performance culture

Performance management flourishes in a high performance culture and it can make a major contribution to creating one. A high performance culture was described by Armstrong (2015) as one in which the pursuit and attainment of demanding performance goals permeates everything that the organization does.

A study on 'Building the high-performance workforce' by the Corporate Leadership Council (2002) led to ten conclusions:

1   The drivers of on-the-job performance are notably different from the drivers of recruiting and retention.

2   The most effective drivers of employee performance are often underemphasized (even excluded) from 'performance management' as it is traditionally defined. Organizations must redefine performance management to include all relevant organizational, managerial and employee-level drivers.

3   No one category of performance management is singularly important. The most effective performance management strategy is composed of a portfolio of carefully selected organizational, managerial and employee-related levers.

4   Employees perform best when they feel personally connected to their work and their organization. These connections are more important to improving employee performance than traditional financial and nonfinancial incentives.

5   Managers can most effectively drive employee performance by providing solutions to day-to-day challenges. Providing employees with informed, positive, fair, accurate and detailed feedback is critical.

6   Organizational factors – systems and culture – have a large impact on employee performance.

7   Communication – between employers, employees and managers, and from senior leadership – stands at the heart of an effective performance management strategy.

8   In order to drive employee performance, organizations should consider careful re-examination of any low-scoring lever. Despite their lesser impact on improving performance, these levers may be crucial to attracting and retaining top talent. In addition, these levers may potentially be redesigned (through more consistent or tailored application) so as to increase their positive impact on performance or enable their support of other higher-impact levers.

9 The impact of performance management levers is remarkably consistent across different segments of the workforce, including geographic region, company, level, function, performance level, and demographic characteristics.

10 The effectiveness of performance management levers varies tremendously, improving or destroying performance by up to 40 per cent. Levers must be chosen and prioritized with precision.

Improving the performance of performance management

The Corporate Executive Board (2012) has identified the following shifts that need to be made to improve the performance of performance management:

- Evolve goal-setting practices. Link individual goals to the organization's priorities; innovate on traditional goal setting practices by 'linking up' to the organization's priorities. Performance goals often fail to produce the right direction and focus; ensure that goals are inspiring enough to generate higher performance.
- Provide employees with the guidance and structure needed to practise new, critical skills in day-to-day work.
- Focus employee performance discussions on the performance itself instead of numerical ratings.
- Feedback that only happens once or twice a year is not enough to help employees to improve. Teach managers to provide feedback and coaching throughout the year.
- Streamline the performance review process. Complex rating processes and lengthy written reviews are time-consuming and frustrating. Scale back documentation requirements and refocus energy on meaningful performance conversations.

Contributions from the iconoclasts

The views of a number of iconoclasts who have been highly critical of performance management as usually practised have made suggestions on how it can be improved. These are summarized below.

Nick Holley

As reported by Janine Milne (2015) Nick Holley, co-director of the Centre for HR Excellence at the UK's Henley Business School has said that: 'The way we currently do performance management, to me, is one of the most destructive things HR has ever created. [It's a way] to reduce employee engagement and really piss off all your managers.' He commented that there actually isn't a right way of doing it. Best practice is 'irrelevant' without context. It's really about organizations individually coming up with a process that works for them, not blindly following the latest management group-think. He believes that performance management should move from being a historical process, looking at past achievements, to how things can be done better in the future. It also means changing it from a negative process of reviewing what people have done well (or failed at), to how people can do better in the future. Rating systems only generate resentment and short-termism. Worse still, as a rating is given a number it's seen as an objective fact, which Holley contends is simply 'rubbish'.

Coens and Jenkins

In their book *Abolishing Performance Appraisals*, Coens and Jenkins (2002) made a strong case against traditional methods of performance appraisal, questioning whether appraisal is necessary and consistent with the work culture espoused by progressive organizations. They do not produce any packaged formula for solving the problem, stating that there are no best practices that you can just copy and implement. Instead they proposed the following seven steps as a means of establishing what will best fit the needs of a particular organization:

1 Conduct a preliminary assessment of the need for change.

2 Approach top management to get a charter that reflects your particular focus and any boundaries of your design process.

3 Form a small design team of passionate stakeholders.

4 Methodically examine the appraisal system you are replacing.

5 Clarify the overall objective for your alternative systems.

6 Develop an alternative set of underlying assumptions.

7 Develop a new design.

Samuel Colbert

Samuel Colbert wrote in *Get Rid of the Performance Review* (2010) that it was time to finally put the performance review out of its misery. His remedy was to replace the one-side-accountable/subordinate-received performance review with a two-sided, reciprocally accountable performance *preview*. His argument was that a performance preview approach gets rid of the quest for faults and instead focuses on joint discussions on how the best use can be made of the individual's skills.

Requirements for success

Armstrong and Baron

Research by Armstrong and Baron (1998; 2005) confirmed that what mattered was not so much the design of the system (which can reproduce the standard performance management model without too much difficulty) but getting the system implemented and working well on a continuing basis. The three key factors affecting the quality of implementation and operation they identified were, first, the commitment, encouragement and support of senior management – the behaviour of management indicates how important performance management is and will therefore strongly influence how it is implemented. Support from top management will be forthcoming if they believe or are persuaded to believe that there is a business case for performance management as a means of delivering increased organizational effectiveness.

The second success factor is the involvement of line managers in developing the scheme and the quality of communications, training, guidance and advice provided to them. Involving line managers in the design of the system and thoroughly communicating to them its purpose, significance and methods of operation will help to gain their commitment. Training is an obvious way to overcome the lack of skill often displayed by line managers, but it is not an easy solution: it demands time and effort. Typically, a new or revised system is launched with a half-day or at most a whole-day briefing and training session that can only touch the surface. There are strong arguments for providing a suite of one-day learning events, one serving as a general introduction to performance management and others dealing separately with each of the main skills managers have to use, namely: goal setting, providing feedback, conducting performance reviews and coaching. These should be supplemented by individual coaching. Organizations are often unwilling to allocate much time to training or coaching but unless they do, performance management will never live up to its expectations.

The third factor is the rigour with which the organization evaluates the effectiveness of performance management and its determination to put things right, often through training. The evaluation of how well performance management is working in practice can provide valuable evidence of the need for improvement – generally or in the skills of individual managers.

Lawler and colleagues

Research conducted by Lawler *et al* (2012) led to the overall conclusion that:

> What organizations need to do is to create performance management systems that are integrated with the other human resource management systems they have and the overall talent management strategy of the organization. Indeed, they need to go beyond just integrating it with the talent management practices of the organization; they need to make sure it is integrated with the strategy of the organization. There has always been, and our data say there continues to be, a strong correlation between the effectiveness of performance management systems and the degree to which they are driven by the business strategy of the organization.

Haines and St-Onge

Haines and St-Onge (2012) established through their research that performance management is most likely to be successful when:

- more performance management training in coaching and giving constructive feedback is provided;
- employee recognition is emphasized;
- the corporate culture values engagement;
- performance management is strategically integrated with human resource management and the business plans of the organization;
- human capital is valued;
- there is a positive employee relations climate.

They also noted that: 'Performance management effectiveness is not only a function of system design or best practices, but also of programme implementation and execution in different organizational contexts.'

Biron and colleagues

Research by Biron *et al* (2011) identified four performance management facilitators: 1) taking a broad view of performance management that includes both strategic and tactical elements; 2) involving senior managers in the process; 3) clearly communicating performance expectations; and 4) formally training performance raters.

Mone and London

Mone and London (2010) pointed out that trust provides a necessary foundation for performance management. Managers must endeavour to create a climate of trust by acting as advocates for their employees, showing confidence and interest in them, being open with them, and acting with integrity (doing what they say they will do).

Suggestions from practitioners

The following is a selection of the eminently practical suggestions made by respondents to the e-reward survey (2014) of performance management (PM):

'Train, communicate, evaluate PM through employee engagement surveys, have HR business partners work with line managers, organize round tables (calibration), provide details of expected competency levels per job type/level, clarify that good is acceptable (not everyone can be a star), encourage on-going performance management, it's more than just an annual administrative hoop – it's a powerful management tool.'

'Train front-line managers on leadership skills and performance management improvement skills. Senior management should demonstrate commitment to the process. Celebrate success and communicate it widely across the organization.'

'Work out why the organization wants to have a PM system. If the decision is to introduce or change the PM system then make sure that the way it works reflects the organization culture. Integrate the PM system with other HR information systems.'

'Make sure that you advise everyone that you plan to introduce the scheme and let employees know "what is in it for them" as well as how it will be managed.'

'Keep it very, very simple, be able to translate strategy to individual goals and give people a clear line of sight, ensure all people managers are capable to deliver PM, eg have a performance dialogue (this is the key!) at any time and not just at the annual review.'

'Gain the support of senior people in the organization, do a lot of prep work including consultation with staff and managers to find out what kind of performance management system would work in this particular environment. Once agreed, really invest in regular training and revision of how the process works.'

'Focus on the positives, create a culture of continual performance management rather than restricting it to an annual appraisal (to avoid surprises when it comes to ratings and encourage individuals to focus on performance throughout the year). Make a performance management system open and available all year round rather than releasing an appraisal at certain set times of the year. Analyse the data on performance ratings, to see trends, highlight areas for improvement and ensure no discriminatory bias. Train.'

'Ensure the paperwork (hardcopy or e-) does not drive the process. The appraisal should be clearly aligned to the organization's strategic objectives and values. It is the conversation between the manager and employee that is most important. Managers need to be given the skills to manage difficult conversations and all staff need to know how to give and receive feedback.'

'Ensure all staff understand how their contribution is measured.'

'Think about what you want from any performance management approach – why have it at all? Listen to feedback from your business owners/shareholders, senior management and staff/employee representatives, decide on the things that will make a difference to your business in the next five years and design your solution to meet that need. Remember, designing a system which picks out the best and worst can ignore the majority who become disenfranchised with PM. Design it to engage the majority as this creates value.'

'Spend most time on consulting/communicating, particularly with the managers expected to do it, rather than on a clever "design".'

'Plan-apply-collect feedback-update.'

'Need to gain employee buy in.'

'Make it simple. Be prepared to challenge managers who avoid difficult decisions/giving feedback (including praise) where required.'

'Keep it simple and easy to understand. If changing an existing scheme, review what is wrong with current system before designing a new one. Time may be better spent embedding the existing one than changing it. Ensure system is backed up with regular performance discussions, not just a discussion once or twice a year.'

'Keep it practical, pragmatic yet professional; ensure differentiation of ratings through forced distribution, include 360 feedback, conduct calibration sessions and demand line managers get trained up.'

'Involve line managers in the design phase, asking what works and doesn't. Keep it simple. Explain the process to the whole work force. Let line managers own the process.'

'Get senior management to support you, otherwise it won't work. All the effort will be wasted. The biggest success factor is based on how it's rolled out.'

'Get senior management buy in to the process as any change needs to be driven from the top. Design your system and run this by employee focus groups as they will tell you what they like and don't like about your system. Use the feedback to improve the system. The employee focus group staff are more likely to champion the system as they have been instrumental in developing it, which helps with engagement.'

'Ensure visibility at all stages – clear line of sight and clear understanding of expectations and outcomes.'

'Ensure the system isn't hampered by bureaucracy and tedious paperwork. Make it easy for all to actively engage with the system and put the focus on having quality open conversation between reviewer and reviewee.'

'Consult employees to understand what motivates them to improve their performance, and what de-motivates them.'

'Consistency – one scheme for all, make it about good conversations, not just a process.'

'Clear line of sight between objective setting, performance review and business goals. Regularly review and update in accordance with any changes in business needs.'

'Be transparent; autonomy for line management (under fixed budget).'

'Be clear about what you are trying to achieve and how you will measure/evaluate whether you have achieved the aims. Have clear strategies and processes for dealing with poor performance and ensure managers are trained in how to deal with poor performance. Create a climate where implementing performance management systems is an absolutely necessary part of a manager's role and a real requirement of the job.'

'Assess what are the objectives/priorities for your organization. Do some benchmarking and best practice but always link back to what will work for your organization right now. Review the process: what was right a few years ago may now need changing.'

'Align your organization's goals and objective to department and individual goals. It's important for employees to understand how their role directly creates value to the organization. This creates transparency and increases motivation among employees.'

'Acknowledge any link to remuneration – if you don't, people will create their own links.'

'Link it consistently to the culture that you want to achieve.'

'Simplicity is beautiful.'

Conclusions

The effective practices referred to in this chapter can be summarized as a set of guidelines given in Table 3.1.

Note that these are *guidelines* only, not 'best practice' prescriptions. How they apply, if they apply at all, is a matter of interpretation taking into account the circumstances of the organization, especially its culture.

It is remarkable that the reputation of performance management is so abysmal in spite of all the good advice upon which these guidelines have been based, some of which has been around for over 20 years. No doubt some organizations get it right, as is shown by the

Table 3.1   Performance management guidelines

1	Guarantee the commitment, encouragement and support of senior management.
2	Involve line managers and employees in developing the scheme.
3	Provide managers with high quality communications, training, guidance and advice.
4	Set clear aims and measurable success criteria for the performance management system.
5	Streamline the performance management process: it should be simple to understand and operate.
6	Emphasize development leading to improved performance.
7	Ensure that the process involves the alignment of individual and organizational goals.
8	Ensure that throughout the year managers hold performance conversations with their team members involving feedback and coaching (abolish the once/twice-a-year performance review).
9	Focus employee performance discussions on the performance itself instead of numerical ratings.
10	Evaluate the effectiveness of performance management.

views expressed by the e-reward respondents quoted earlier. Many haven't, however, as is evidenced by the research, and the recent surge of new approaches to performance management is an indication of dissatisfaction with the status quo. The advice is there but the extent to which it has been taken is limited. This is presumably because of complacency (only two-fifths of the respondents to the e-reward, 2014, performance management survey had formally evaluated their performance management system), ignorance, reluctance to change or inability to affect changes.

Many of the commentators referred to in this chapter have rightly emphasized that there is no such thing as best practice performance management – no universal solutions. What works in one environment will not necessarily work elsewhere. The many-faceted and demanding nature of performance management is a problem. Cascio (2010) commented that: 'It is an exercise in observation and judgement, it is a feedback process, it is an organizational intervention. It is a measurement process as well as an intensely emotional process. Above all, it is an inexact, human process.' Getting it right by heeding the advice is hard, but something does need to be done about it, as has been recognized by a number of organizations referred to in the next chapter.

References

Armstrong, M (2015) *Handbook of Performance Management*, 5th edn, Kogan Page, London

Armstrong, M and Baron, A (1998) *Performance Management: The new realities*, CIPD, London

Armstrong, M and Baron, A (2005) *Managing Performance: Performance management in action*, CIPD, London

Biron, M, Farndale, E and Paauwe, J (2011) Performance management effectiveness: lessons from world-leading firms, *International Journal of Human Resource Management*, 22 (6), pp 1294–311

Cascio, W F (2010) *Managing Human Resources: Productivity, quality of work life, profits*, 8th edn, McGraw-Hill Irwin, New York

Coens, T and Jenkins, M (2002) *Abolishing Performance Appraisals: Why they backfire and what to do instead*, Berrett-Koehler, San Francisco, CA

Colbert, S A (2010) *Get Rid of the Performance Review*, Hachette, New York

Corporate Executive Board (2012) Driving breakthrough performance in the new work environment, CEB, Arlington, VA

Corporate Leadership Council (2002) http://talentexperiment.com/images/ CLC_Building_the_High_Performance_Workforce_A_Quantitative_ Analysis_of_the_Effectiveness_of_Performance_Management_ Strategies_1_.pdf (accessed 20 January 2016)

Egan, G (1995) A clear path to peak performance, *People Management*, 18 May, pp 34–37

e-reward (2014) *Survey of Performance Management*, e-reward, Stockport

Folger, R and Cropanzano, R (1998) *Organizational Justice and Human Resource Management*, Sage, Thousand Oaks, CA

Folger, R, Konovsky, M A and Cropanzano, R (1992) A due process metaphor for performance appraisal, in (eds) B M Staw and L L Cummings, *Research in Organizational Behavior*, JAI Press, Greenwich, CT

Haines, V Y and St-Onge, S (2012) Performance management effectiveness: practices or context? *International Journal of Human Resource Management*, **23** (6), pp 1158–75

Lawler, E E, Benson, G S and McDermott, M (2012) What makes performance appraisals effective? *Compensation & Benefits Review*, **44** (4), pp 191–200

Milne, J (2015) Performance management – the 'soul-sucking monster' of HR, http://diginomica.com/author/jmilne/ (accessed 21 February 2016)

Mone, E M and London, M (2010) *Employee Engagement through Performance Management: A practical guide for managers*, Routledge, New York

Pulakos, E D, Mueller-Hanson, R A and O'Leary, R S (2008) Performance management in the US, in (eds) A Varma, P S Budhwar and A DeNisi, *Performance Management Systems: A global perspective*, Routledge, Abingdon

Sparrow, P and Hiltrop, J M (1994) *European Human Resource Management in Transition*, Prentice Hall, Harlow

Strebler, M T, Bevan, S and Robertson D (2001) *Performance Review: Balancing objectives and content*, Institute for Employment Studies, Brighton

Taylor, M S, Tracy, K B, Renard, M K, Harrison, J K and Carroll, S J (1995) Due process in performance appraisal: a quasi-experiment in procedural justice, *Administrative Science Quarterly*, **40**, pp 495–523

Winstanley, D and Stuart-Smith, K (1996) Policing performance: the ethics of performance management, *Personnel Review*, **25** (6), pp 66–84

What's happening to performance management?

04

Organizations have recently been looking very hard at their performance management systems and haven't liked what they have seen. The e-reward survey (2014) established that there was generally less focus on bureaucracy and form-filling exercises and more on performance management becoming an on-going process and part of the company's culture. Here are three examples of the steps respondents were taking:

> 'We removed the need for individuals to be awarded a performance rating, eg exceptional, good, poor, etc. The link to a non-consolidated pay award was also removed.'

> 'Moved from a forced distribution system to more qualitative developmental discussions.'

> 'Focus on conversations, moving away from a forced distribution curve. Aim is to engage our people, build trust and leverage greater potential value from the conversation and the approach to performance management.'

In the United States many businesses have been making significant changes to their performance management systems. Here are six examples.

Examples of changes to performance management systems

Adobe

Adobe, the computer software company based in California, has 13,000 employees. It flourishes in a highly competitive industry. The company's founding values are to be genuine, exceptional, innovative and involved. Attempts had been made over five years to realign its performance management system to these values but it had failed. It was estimated that managers were spending 80,000 hours a year on it.

It was decided to introduce an entirely new system, the features of which were:

- no ratings, no prescribed format, no forms, no technology 'system';
- the annual review meeting was replaced by manager and employee 'check-ins' covering expectations, feedback, growth and development agenda, to be whenever sensible but at least quarterly;
- extensive training support was provided for managers – role plays, lectures and online;
- an employee support centre was established;
- managers were made entirely responsible for managing their pay budgets and pay outcomes and allocated budgets;
- managers were able to define their own processes and requirements for HR support;
- regular pulse surveys were held to measure engagement and provide insights on decisions and impact.

The outcome was that the focus was no longer on process, chasing numbers and ratings. Frequent feedback was provided in the regular check-ins (average one a month per employee). The new currency for employees and managers – feedback – was no longer feared, managers' knowledge of performance of individuals was significantly greater than ever before, and the demand for training on coaching others, handling difficult conversations, mentoring, career development and managing reward increased. Levels of engagement increased and voluntary turnover decreased by 30 per cent in two years.

Accenture

Pierre Nanterme, CEO of Accenture, a global professional services firm with 33,000 employees, explained what was happening to performance management in his company (*Washington Post*, 2015):

> We're going to get rid of it. Not 100 per cent, but we're going to get rid of probably 90 per cent of what we did in the past. It's not what we need. We are not sure that spending all that time on performance management has been yielding a great outcome.
>
> And for the millennium generation, it's not the way they want to be recognized, the way they want to be measured. If you put this new generation in the box of the performance management we've used the last 30 years, you lose them... All this terminology of rankings – forcing rankings along some distribution curve or whatever – we're done with that. We've totally done too much effort for a limited outcome. We're going to evaluate you in your role, not vis-á-vis someone else who might work in Washington, who might work in Bangalore. It's irrelevant. It should be about you. How are you performing now, and do we believe you are prepared to move to another role? We are getting rid of all this comparison with other people.

Deloitte

As reported by Marcus Buckingham and Ashley Goodall (2015), a complete redesign of the Deloitte performance management system was undertaken because it was believed that the current approach was completely out of step with the firm's objectives. A further incentive to change was provided by a survey which revealed that 58 per cent of its executives failed to drive either employee engagement or high performance.

In the typical existing performance management system, objectives were set for each of the 65,000-plus employees at the beginning of the year and each of them were rated for each completed project (the work is mainly project-based) on how well the objectives were met. These evaluations were factored into a single year-end rating, arrived at in lengthy 'consensus meetings' at which groups of 'counsellors' discussed hundreds of people, comparing them with their peers.

As part of the research conducted before planning a new approach, Deloitte counted the number of hours the organization spent on performance management and found that completing the forms, holding the meetings, and creating the ratings consumed close to 2 million hours a year. Many of those hours were spent by leaders discussing the outcomes of the process. As Buckingham and Goodall remarked: 'We wondered if we could somehow shift our investment of time from talking to ourselves about ratings to talking to our people about their performance and careers – from a focus on the past to a focus on the future.'

A review of research on ratings was conducted from which it was discovered that ratings were determined mainly by the peculiarity of the perceptions of raters rather than by actual performance, and that ratings of skills were particularly prone to error. Finally, internal research was conducted to establish the validity of a 'strengths-based' approach to performance management. A total of 60 high-performing teams with 1,287 employees were identified and a control group of 1,954 employees was set up. A six-item survey was conducted which revealed that three items correlated best with high performance for a team: 'My co-workers are committed to doing quality work', 'The mission of our company inspires me', and 'I have the chance to use my strengths every day.' Of these, the third was the most powerful across the organization.

This evidence indicated that a quick way had to be found to collect reliable and differentiated performance data. It was also necessary to develop an approach that would provide for more time to be spent on helping people to use their strengths in teams characterized by clarity of purpose and expectations.

The system then developed by Deloitte was characterized by speed, agility, one-size-fits-one, and constant learning. It was underpinned by a new way of collecting reliable performance data. It has no cascading objectives, no once-a-year reviews, and no 360-degree-feedback tools.

It was decided that the three main objectives of the new system would be, first, to *recognize performance*, particularly through variable compensation. However, to recognize performance it is necessary to see it clearly: the second objective was therefore to *measure performance*. This raised two issues: the 'idiosyncratic rater effect' and the need to streamline the traditional rating process. The solution to this evaluation issue was to get team leaders to pose very different questions to their team members. Note was taken of the fact that while people may rate other people's skills inconsistently, they are highly consistent when rating their own feelings and intentions. It was therefore decided to get team leaders to decide on what future actions they wanted taken for each of their team members rather than rate their skills. At the end of every project (or once every quarter for long-term projects) team leaders are asked to respond to the following four future-focused statements about each of their team members:

1 Given what I know of this person's performance, and if it were my money, I would award this person the highest possible compensation increase and bonus *(measures overall performance and unique value to the organization on a five-point scale from 'strongly agree' to 'strongly disagree').*

2 Given what I know of this person's performance, I would always want him or her on my team *(measures ability to work well with others on the same five-point scale).*

3 This person is at risk for low performance *(identifies problems that might harm the customer or the team on a yes or no basis).*

4 This person is ready for promotion today *(measures potential on a yes or no basis).*

In effect, team leaders are asked what they would *do* with each team member rather than what they *think* of that individual. These data points are aggregated over a year, and weighted according to the duration of a given project, to produce a rich stream of information for leaders' discussions of what they, in turn, will do – whether it's a question of succession planning, development paths, or performance-pattern analysis. Once a quarter the organization's leaders can use the new data to review a targeted subset of employees (those eligible for promotion, for example, or those with critical skills) and can debate what actions Deloitte might take to better develop that particular group. This method of evaluation could be regarded as a rating, but it bears no resemblance to the ratings of the past. Because it enables the rapid capture of performance at a single moment, it is called a 'performance snapshot'.

The third objective was to *fuel performance*. Research into the practices of the best team leaders in Deloitte revealed that they conduct regular check-ins with each team member about current work. These brief conversations allow leaders to set expectations for the upcoming week, review priorities, comment on recent work, and provide correction, coaching, or important new information, and clarify what is expected of the team member and why, what great work looks like, and how the best work can be accomplished. This constitutes the trinity of purpose, expectations and strengths that characterizes the best teams in Deloitte.

Every team leader is required to check in with each team member once a week. These check-ins are not *in addition* to the work of a team leader; they *are* the work of a team leader. There was a direct and measurable correlation between the frequency of these conversations and the engagement of team members. However, team leaders have many demands on their time and it was established that the best way to ensure frequency was to have check-ins initiated by the team member – who more often than not is eager for the guidance and attention they provide – rather than by the team leader.

Gap Inc

In 2014, Gap Inc launched a new performance management process for its headquarters' employees worldwide: GPS – 'Grow. Perform. Succeed'. The company is also introducing a slightly modified version of GPS for its retail store and distribution centre staff. As Rob Ollander-Krane, Senior Director, Organization Performance Effectiveness at Gap Inc, who devised the new scheme, commented: 'We really wanted to drive performance and engage our employees and I don't think that a once-a-year, mostly administrative process that's tied to a fixed distribution curve can do that.' Gone are the formal reviews and performance ratings of the past – instead, managers and employees are encouraged to have 12 informal, undocumented conversations (called 'touch base' meetings) about performance over the course of the year. Gap believes that GPS has 'repurposed' thousands of working hours and millions of dollars from tasks that did not drive performance to discussions that do. What's more, staff surveys suggest employees feel that the new process is providing them with better feedback, offering more opportunities to learn and driving them to higher levels of performance.

A full case study on the new approach to performance management at Gap Inc is given in Appendix A.

IBM

The impetus for changing the performance management system at IBM was the realization that IBM employees were doing work differently from the way the system assumed. This involved the setting and review of annual objectives, but during the year new requirements frequently arise, which means that employees are not necessarily working towards what was originally listed as an annual objective. The result was that they would end up in an irrelevant discussion in December, trying to assess whether they had fulfilled the goals they'd drafted 11 months earlier.

A post on IBM's internal social media platform was used to crowd-source the views of IBM's 380,000 employees in 170 countries. The post received 75,000 views and 2,000 comments from employees. Employees said that they wanted to receive feedback more frequently. They rejected the idea of self-assessment and objected to relative performance rankings in which managers met with one another and compared their employees.

The end result was a new app-based performance review system called Checkpoint. This enables employees to set shorter-term goals, and managers will provide feedback on their progress at least every quarter. At the end of the year, employees will be judged across five criteria – business results, impact on client success, innovation, personal responsibility to others, and skills. Managers will assess whether employees have exceeded or achieved expectations for their role in each of those five dimensions or if there's a need for improvement.

The single measure of an employee's performance that used to obsess everyone has been abolished. The five scores in the new system lead to a richer, more balanced discussion.

Microsoft

In 2013, Microsoft removed its previous system of performance management which involved an annual formal performance review and used a process known as 'stack ranking' to divide employees into five performance categories along a targeted distribution of ratings. Instead, an approach was adopted that focuses on collaboration, feedback and rewards for impact. To emphasize the importance of personal development the new approach is referred to as 'performance and development' rather than 'performance management'.

The formal annual performance review was replaced by less formal but regular performance and development conversations between managers and employees, called 'Connects'. Every employee is expected to have a minimum of two Connects a year – but beyond this, Microsoft does not apply any strict rules. Ratings were abolished. Employees identified their priorities rather than setting objectives.

As Microsoft's Director of Global Performance Programmes, Lisa Dodge, explained to the e-reward researcher:

> The outcome of the old end-of-year review usually felt like a judgement, rather than an opportunity for employees to learn and get better. The focus of our current approach is designed to help people deliver great impact by working together, reflecting and getting feedback more often, and more intentionally considering learning and growing – and as a result deliver continually better business results. Regular performance conversations have been separated from the reward conversations. Instead of the end-of-year review, managers and employees have a short reward discussion to share the merit, bonus and stock outcomes with the employee. Meanwhile, the regular discussions employees and managers have during the year focus on the impact someone is having, what they are learning and what they can do in the upcoming few months – there is no discussion of rewards.

Lisa Dodge also observed that:

> With the old system people were too distracted by their rating. Under the new approach, they are able to more fully appreciate their rewards... Our employees don't need ratings to know how they are doing... We want rich conversations rather than assuming an employee's performance can be boiled down to a simple label.

A full case study on the new approach to performance management at Microsoft is given in Appendix B.

Conclusions

The common thread running through all these case studies is disillusion with the relevance and effectiveness of formal performance reviews and their replacement with more frequent and less formal conversations about progress and development between managers and individuals, called variously check-ins, touch-base meetings, connects, performance snapshots or performance and development conversations. Traditional overall ratings were abolished in five of the six cases.

References

Buckingham, M and Goodall, A (2015) Reinventing performance management, *Harvard Business Review*, April, pp 40–50

e-reward (2014) *Survey of Performance Management*, e-reward, Stockport

Washington Post (2015) https://www.washingtonpost.com/news/on-leadership/wp/2015/07/23/accenture-ceo-explains-the-reasons-why-hes-overhauling-performance-reviews/ (accessed 20 April 2016)

Performance management – the issues

05

A good case for reinventing performance management was made in a study conducted by the Society for Human Resource Management (quoted by Coens and Jenkins, 2002). The study revealed that more than 90 per cent of appraisal schemes were unsuccessful. No doubt some performance management schemes work well but many don't. Line managers are often given the blame for failure but the real problem is the system and how it is planned, implemented and operated.

Systemic problems as described in Chapter 2 can only be resolved by a comprehensive review of the issues involved as the basis for fundamental changes, in other words, reinventing the system. The main issues that have to be addressed are listed below and discussed in more detail later in the chapter. The chapter ends with an analysis of the role of HR in performance management and an indication of how the issues can be dealt with. Succeeding chapters deal with approaches to reinvention in each of the key aspects of performance management.

The issues

1   Lack of commitment and support from top management.
2   Over-engineered complex systems designed by HR that demand more from line managers than they can reasonably be expected to do.

3   Over-emphasis on setting quantified 'SMART' objectives and not aligning individual objectives to the organization's goals.

4   Focus on the dishonest annual ritual of a once-a-year performance review or appraisal meeting, thus neglecting the essential feature of performance management – that it is an on-going process that should take place throughout the year.

5   Reliance on ratings and, in some cases, forced rankings that only serve to demotivate people.

6   The stated or implicit belief that performance management only exists to generate ratings that inform performance-related pay decisions.

7   Insufficient emphasis on development and linking performance management to talent management.

8   Little attention given to the education and training of managers in why performance management is important and their role in implementing it.

9   Poor implementation.

10 Inadequate evaluation.

1 Top management commitment and support

The role of top management is to manage performance. The chief executive, with the support of the top management team, sets goals, formulates strategies to achieve the goals and ensures that these strategies are implemented. The whole top management team is there to create and maintain a high performance culture, one in which the values, norms and practices of an organization combine to create a climate in which the achievement of high levels of performance is a way of life. As defined by Armstrong (2014), the characteristics of a high performance culture are:

• Management affirms and re-affirms what it expects in the shape of levels of performance and performance improvements, sets goals for success and monitors performance to ensure that the goals are achieved.

- A clear line of sight exists between the strategic aims of the organization and those of its departments and its employees at all levels.

- Work practices such as smart working, lean manufacturing, flexible working, job redesign, autonomous work teams, improvement groups and team briefing are adopted.

- People know what's expected of them – they understand their goals and accountabilities.

- People feel that their job is worth doing, and there is a strong fit between the job and their capabilities.

- People are empowered to maximize their contribution.

- There is strong leadership from the top which engenders a shared belief in the importance of continuing improvement.

- There is a focus on promoting positive attitudes that result in an engaged, committed and motivated workforce.

- Performance management processes are aligned to business goals.

- The capacities of people are developed through learning at all levels to support performance improvement and they are provided with opportunities to make full use of their skills and abilities.

- A pool of talent ensures a continuous supply of high performers in key roles.

- People are valued and rewarded according to their contribution.

- People are involved in developing high performance practices.

- There is a climate of trust and teamwork, aimed at delivering a distinctive service to the customer.

These are all matters that concern members of the top management team. They have to promote a performance culture, oversee the development of the performance management system, ensure that line managers are aware of the importance attached to performance management. and lead by example, ie put into practice performance management processes with their own staff.

HR also has the vital role of encouraging and supporting top management. Their job is not simply to design the system. They have to make out the business case for performance management and they have to make great efforts in conjunction with senior management to see that it works. They will only be able to do this if they understand the business model of the organization and the factors that deliver the results required by that model. They need to know what good performance looks like and how to ensure that it happens.

2 Complexity

Willing participation in performance management activities is more likely to be achieved if managers do not see it as a bureaucratic chore. If forms are used they should be as simple as possible: no more than two sides of one piece of paper. Web-enabled performance management eliminates paperwork and can speed up the process, but it must not be too complicated. It should be emphasized that performance management is not a form-filling, box-ticking or data-entry exercise and that the important thing is the dialogue between managers and individuals that continues throughout the year. It is not just an annual event.

One problem with the standard model of performance management, as illustrated in Figure 1.2 (see page 23) is that it can encourage an over-elaborate approach. Systems designers may be tempted to cover every aspect of the model in detail and turn what should be a natural and straightforward management process into a bureaucratic nightmare with complex procedures and intricate paper- or computer-based forms. Managers don't like this and won't do it properly, if at all. Employees generally regard it as yet another control mechanism imposed from above.

As noted in Chapter 2, too much complexity is built into the system when performance reviews are expected to fulfil numerous functions including performance improvement, feedback, coaching, goal setting, skill development, the identification of potential, pay determination and the identification of under-performers. As Mueller-Hanson and Pulakos (2012) observed: 'PM approaches that try to serve too many purposes will not serve any purpose well.' When designing the system it is best to focus the scope of performance reviews on a limited range of functions, eg goal setting, feedback and development planning.

The watchwords are 'keep it simple'. Limit forms, if they are used at all, to no more than two pages. Computerize any recording required but again, resist the temptation to load the process with a multitude of tick boxes.

Avoid jargon. Terms such as 'role profile', 'key result areas' or 'key performance indicators' make perfect sense to HR as explanations of how the system works. To the managers and employees who have to run the system they can look like prime examples of 'managerese' or HR-speak. Such terms should be avoided or at least minimized in communications about the scheme or during training. My experience as a practitioner, consultant and researcher has shown that this can be achieved without prejudicing the effectiveness of the system as long as the basic processes of goal setting, feedback and development planning are covered.

3 Objectives

There are three issues relating to setting objectives: an over-emphasis on quantification, the use of the 'SMART' acronym, and linking individual and organizational objectives.

Over-emphasis on quantification

A performance objective or goal (the terms are interchangeable) describes what someone has to accomplish. Ideally objectives should be defined as specific targets – eg 'reduce reject levels by 3 per cent within nine months', 'introduce x by y'. The problem is that, as a hangover from the largely discredited management by objectives system, some organizations insist that all objectives should be quantified in this way. For some jobs or parts of jobs where the job-holder is responsible for providing advice this can be difficult. For example, HR business partners are there, amongst other things, to provide advice and support to their line manager clients. A quantified target of, say: 'Provide a minimum of five pieces of good advice a week' would be meaningless, but it is possible to define the conditions that would exist if the task of providing advice has been well done, for example: 'The advisory aspect of the job will have been done well when the job holder consistently provides prompt, good and action-able advice to line manager clients as required.' This can be termed a 'standard of performance'. Unless this is practised when appropriate, line managers will be frustrated by having to pursue the will-of-the-wisp of quantification for the sake of quantification.

Use of the SMART acronym

The acronym SMART is often used to define a good performance objective or goal. Traditionally, S stands for specific (sometimes stretching), M for measurable, A for agreed, R for realistic and T for time-related. But an emphasis on being SMART may give managers the impression that everything has to be quantified, which leads to frustration when they find out that it can't be done and results in the setting of unrealistic targets.

As Chamberlin (2011) argued, the real aim of setting goals is for people to know: what they have to do, when they've done it, that they are able to do it, why they have to do it (ie who for), that it is something they should be doing, and how they are progressing along the way. He criticized the conventional acronym and suggested that the last three letters of the mnemonic should be amended to read A for attainable, R for relevant and T for trackable. Chamberlin attached particular importance to *relevant* – the goal has to be linked to the business and its customers. He also emphasized *trackable* because the important thing to do with goals is to monitor progress over time, ie track them. He rejected *time-related* because it did not convey this essential feature and was in any case covered already by *specific*.

Linking individual and organizational objectives

The textbooks on performance management usually recommend that it should be linked to the organization's priorities, but they do not make it clear how this can be done. It is hard. Individual roles can seem to be remote from the organization's goals. Where the attempt is made to establish a link it can too easily be expressed as a bland declaration of intent rather than a specific objective. Only half the respondents to e-reward's performance management survey (2014) said they did it. But it can be done, as described in the next chapter.

4 Annual performance reviews

There has been almost universal agreement amongst commentators with the observation by Gabriella Jozwiak (2012) that:

> Every workplace has its idiosyncratic seasonal events, and HR is perhaps most visible during the annual performance appraisal. Why? Because employees dislike them. They are time-consuming, involve too much paperwork, HR would even do better to drop them altogether and find a better performance-management tool.

She quoted a recent US poll of 2,677 people (1,800 employees, 645 HR managers and 232 CEOs) by Achievers, the San Francisco-based rewards and recognition consulting firm, which revealed that 98 per cent of staff found annual performance reviews unnecessary. Replacing the annual review with more frequent feedback conversations during the course of the year has been perhaps the biggest change made by organizations that have reinvented their performance management systems. How this can take place is discussed in Chapter 7.

5 Rating and forced ranking

The reconsideration of performance rating, and the use of forced ranking systems is another major feature of the new approach to performance management. The issues involved are described more thoroughly in Chapter 8.

Rating

Rating involves the assessment by a reviewer of the level of performance of an employee expressed on a scale, frequently alphabetic or numerical. On the basis of research conducted by the Institute for Employment Studies, Wendy Hirsh and her colleagues (2011) noted that:

> The performance rating aspect of PM was not seen as motivating by most of those involved in the research, especially as it tells most people they are satisfactory, which is not very exciting news and mildly demotivating. Some employees would like a rating scale with more points, but this seems likely to generate more dissatisfaction. Performance rating is

also seen as unfair because objectives vary in difficulty and managers in how they assess.

Rating sometimes involves forced ranking or forced distribution.

Forced ranking

Forced ranking requires managers to place their staff in order, from best to worst. The rank order is divided into predetermined categories expressed as percentiles that are defined as a hierarchy of performance grades. Individuals are then placed in one of those grades according to their rank order.

The following criticism of forced ranking was made by Pfeffer and Sutton (2006):

> We couldn't find a shred of evidence that it is better to have just a few alpha dogs at the top and treat everyone else as inferior. Rather, the best performance comes in organizations where as many people as possible are treated as top dogs. If you want people to keep working together and keep earning together, it is better to grant prestige to many rather than few, and to avoid big gaps between who gets the most rewards and kudos.

This and many other criticisms of forced ranking coupled with the bad experiences of it in companies such as Microsoft and the fact that the use of forced ranking did not prevent Enron from imploding, have combined to produce widespread revulsion for the practice. Even though a reinvented performance management system may keep some form of rating, it is unlikely to retain forced ranking.

Forced distribution

A forced distribution system does not involve ranking but does require managers to conform to a laid down distribution of performance ratings, for example, the highest level performers would be placed in category A, the middle 70 per cent would have to be placed in category B and the remaining 15 per cent would be placed in category C. Forced distribution systems are often imposed to ensure that ratings are spread in an acceptable proportion over each performance category, thus preventing tendencies such as putting too high a proportion of ratings in the central category (a fairly common practice) or skewing ratings to the higher categories. This is a procrustean process that achieves a sort of artificial order but assumes that the distribution of performance is the same everywhere, which cannot be the case. Managers and their staff generally dislike it.

6 Performance management and performance-related pay

It is often assumed the performance-related pay schemes can only function when there is a rating process that determines the size of the increase. It is true that most organizations with performance pay base it on ratings, but 20 per cent of the respondents to the e-reward performance management survey (2014) did not and there are ways in which pay decisions can be made without them, as described in Chapter 9.

The other issue is whether the rating and performance pay decisions should take place at the same time or whether they should be separated – 'decoupled'. Separating them may be favoured because it helps to ensure that the developmental components of the review, such as performance improvement and identifying training needs, are not prejudiced by concerns over pay outcomes. Nearly two-fifths of the respondents to the e-reward contingent pay survey (2009) conducted them at separate times. As one of them put it: 'The performance review should not become a pay negotiation.' Making performance pay decisions without ratings is discussed in Chapter 8.

7 Employee development and talent management

Conceptually, the prime concern of performance management is the development of people to perform even better in the future and to advance their careers. The Institute for Employment Studies research (Hirsh *et al*, 2011) established that in several of the case organizations, employee development was an important intended purpose of performance management but it was weakly executed compared with objective-setting or performance review. Annual reviews tend to spend most of the time looking backwards, not forwards.

An associated issue is the link between performance management and talent management. This is not always as explicit as it should be. Performance management can support the two key talent management activities of identifying talent and developing talent. It is necessary to ensure that line managers are aware of the part they should play in these activities and are given guidance in carrying out that role.

8 Line managers

Line managers are often blamed for the failure of performance management but the real blame should be attached to those who expect too much of them in handling over-complex systems and fail to provide them with the training, guidance and help they need to develop and apply the demanding skills required. The research conducted by the Institute for Employment Studies (Hirsh *et al*, 2011) found that:

> Training in PM was quite haphazard or cursory in several of the cases. It could be included as a small item in a general introduction to management. Such training often concentrated on how to fill in the forms rather than the purpose of PM or how to have performance and development conversations. Some cases had modules in managing poor performance, but PM training was often not mandatory. Training in PM still tends to the 'sheep dip' approach rather than being tailored to the manager's needs and level of existing expertise.

Approaches to develop the skills and commitment of line managers are described in Chapter 10.

9 Implementing performance management

Organizations introducing performance management or amending an existing scheme start with good intentions. They know what they want to achieve and believe they have the answer to the question 'how should it be achieved'. But intent is not converted into action. The design of the scheme (eg over-complex) and its method of introduction (poor communications or inadequate training) predicate failure. The solution is to 'design with implementation in mind', and ways of doing this are described in Chapter 11.

10 Evaluating performance management

A process as demanding and complex as performance management needs to be evaluated regularly to check that it is functioning as planned and to identify any actions required to improve its effectiveness. Yet only 31 per cent of the respondents to the e-reward 2014 survey of performance management reported that they conducted formal evaluations. Previously, Guest and Conway (1998) commented that it was impossible for them to reach any conclusion on the extent to which performance management improves performance because the survey upon which they were basing their assessment revealed that very few organizations were evaluating their schemes. Evaluation is essential, and methods of doing it are explained in Chapter 11.

The role of HR

At one time, the personnel department tended to be not only the sponsor but also the custodian of performance appraisal schemes. As a result line managers regarded them as the preserve of personnel and therefore not their concern. They went through the motions, but no more. The Institute for Employment Studies (Hirsh *et al*, 2011) stated that: 'The biggest tension in performance management is between managing performance and filling in the paperwork. HR knows it wants the first but can't help itself from emphasizing the second.'

HR should no longer run the performance appraisal scheme like this, but the danger of simply giving it away has to be recognized. The role of HR becomes that of encouraging and facilitating the sort of performance management processes described in this book. This is an important role. HR specialists work alongside line managers, helping them as necessary to develop their skills, encouraging them to carry out their performance management responsibilities and providing guidance on such matters as preparing role profiles, including knowledge, skills and competency analysis. They assemble teams of committed and experienced managers who can act as coaches and mentors and stimulate the creation of communities of practice, ensuring that performance management is on the agenda. More specifically, they run training events and conduct surveys to evaluate the effectiveness of performance management. In essence, HR specialists exist to support performance management rather than drive it. The following comment on the role of HR in performance management is based on research carried out by Armstrong and Ward (2005):

> HR's role in performance management is crucial. They tend to be the people that are in charge of designing and reviewing systems, convincing boards of a new approach, implementing new processes, running workshops for managers and staff, providing advice and support materials to staff and managers, and ensuring there is compliance with the system. However, they cannot be at every appraisal discussion; they can't ensure that managers and employees have 'quality' conversations; and they have a limited ability to improve the capability and engagement of managers in managing performance.

Conclusions

The main issues facing performance management are:

1   Lack of commitment and support from top management.

2   Over-engineered complex systems.

3   Over-emphasis on setting quantified 'SMART' objectives.

4   Focus on the dishonest annual ritual of a once-a-year performance review or appraisal meeting.

5   Reliance on ratings and, in some cases, forced rankings.

6   The belief that performance management only exists to generate ratings that inform performance-related pay decisions.

7   Insufficient emphasis on development and linking performance management to talent management.

8   Little attention given to the education and training of managers in why performance management is important and their role in implementing it.

9 Poor implementation.

10 Inadequate evaluation.

Reinventing performance management means that these issues have to be addressed. Their range and complexity means that this is not an easy task, as is evidenced by the performance management problems that continue to be experienced by many organizations. It is noticeable that the reported reinvention programmes of a number of large organizations have concentrated on only two major issues: the annual performance review and rating.

References

Armstrong M (2014) *A Handbook of Human Resource Management Practice*, 13th edn, Kogan Page, London

Armstrong, K and Ward, A (2005) *What Makes for Effective Performance Management?* The Work Foundation, London

Chamberlin, J (2011) Who put the 'art' in SMART goals? *Management Services*, Autumn, pp 22–27

Coens, T and Jenkins, M (2002) *Abolishing Performance Appraisals: Why they backfire and what to do instead*, Berrett-Koehler, San Francisco, CA

e-reward (2009) *Report on Contingent Pay*, e-reward, Stockport

e-reward (2014) *Survey of Performance Management Practice*, e-reward, Stockport

Guest, D E and Conway, N (1998) An analysis of the results of the IPD performance management survey, in M Armstrong and A Baron, *Performance Management: The new realities*, Institute of Personnel and Development, London

Hirsh, W, Brown, D, Chubb, C and Reilly, P (2011) *Performance Management: The implementation challenge*, Institute for Employment Studies, http://www.employment-studies.co.uk/system/files/resources/files/mp89.pdf (accessed 10 March 2016)

Jozwiak, G (2012) Is it time to give up on performance appraisals?, http://www.hrmagazine.co.uk/article-details/is-it-time-to-give-up-on-performance-appraisals (accessed 10 March 2016)

Mueller-Hanson, R A and Pulakos, E D (2012) Putting the 'performance' back in performance management, http://www.shrm.org:research:documents:shrm-siopperformancemanagement.pdf (accessed 11 March 2016)

Pfeffer, J and Sutton, R I (2006) *Hard Facts, Dangerous Half-Truths and Total Nonsense*, Harvard Business School Press, Cambridge, MA

Improve objective setting

06

Introduction

Setting objectives or goals as the basis for defining the results people should achieve and therefore the direction they should take are traditionally fundamental performance management activities. Objectives are supposed to provide the criteria needed to monitor and measure performance and provide the means through which the organization's strategies can be communicated to employees. Ed Lawler and colleagues (2012) observed that:

> Goals provide a very effective approach to directing individuals to support the business strategy of the organization and can translate strategies from an organizational objective to specific individual behaviours.

But there are a number of issues related to the use of objectives, discussed later in this chapter. However, before addressing them it is necessary to examine in some detail the conceptual background and how, ideally, the process is supposed to work by reference to the criteria for a good objective and the methodology for setting objectives. The extent to which this ideal version is realistic can then be explored and approaches to dealing with any problems discussed.

The conceptual background

A *performance objective* or *goal* defines what someone has to accomplish. Objectives for individuals can be agreed either as targets or standards. A target is a quantified or specific objective; for example:

'increase sales revenue by 5 per cent by next March', 'reduce reject levels by 3 per cent within nine months', 'introduce x by y', 'respond to all incoming queries or complaints within two working days', 'convert x per cent of cold calls into an order'. *Performance standards* are on-going and usually qualitative, indicating the conditions that exist when a task has been well done. For example: 'performance in providing advice to line managers will be up to standard when it is appropriate, timely, accepted and implemented', 'performance as a team leader will be acceptable when the team works well together and delivers the results expected of it', 'performance as a receptionist will be up to standard when visitors are welcomed in a friendly way and dealt with efficiently'.

The conceptual background to the use of goals in performance management is provided by goal theory as first formulated by Latham and Locke (1979), which states that people perform better when they have specific and challenging but reachable goals. Acceptance of goals is achieved when:

- people perceive the goals as fair and reasonable and trust their managers;
- individuals participate in goal setting;
- support is provided by the manager – a supportive manager does not use goals to threaten people but rather to clarify what is expected of them;
- people are provided with the resources required to achieve their goals;
- success is achieved in reaching goals, which reinforces acceptance of future goals.

Locke and Latham (2004) held that specific and challenging goals lead to higher performance than no goals or setting general goals such as 'try your best'. Also people who participate in setting their own goals are likely to set more difficult goals than others will set for them, and goal difficulty leads to increased commitment to achieving the goals. Feedback and competition have a similar effect on performance. Therefore, the extent to which goals lead to high performance depends on participation, commitment and other elements of the performance management process such as feedback. There are benefits arising from goal setting but also problems, as summed up by Latham and Locke (2006); see below.

Benefits and problems of goal setting

Benefits:

- gives a sense of purpose;
- provides an unambiguous basis for judging success;
- increases performance;
- is a means for self-management;
- increases subjective wellbeing.

Potential problems:

- lack of sufficient knowledge for goal attainment;
- goal conflict among group members;
- fear of risk-taking;
- ignoring non-goal dimensions of performance;
- demoralization because, following success, management may set higher, impossible goals.

Alignment

In traditional performance management schemes much importance is rightly attached to the alignment of individual and corporate objectives. Performance management is seen as an important means of ensuring that employees understand what the organization is setting out to do and will direct their efforts towards the achievement of these corporate goals.

Criteria for an effective performance objective

The traditional criteria for an effective performance objective in the form of a target or standard are that it should be:

- *Aligned*: consistent with the goals and values of the organization and supporting their achievement.
- *Relevant*: consistent with the purpose of the role.
- *Precise*: specific, clear and well-defined.
- *Measurable*: related to quantified or qualitative performance measures or standards.
- *Trackable*: progress towards achieving the goal can be monitored.
- *Challenging*: to stimulate high standards of performance and to encourage progress.
- *Achievable*: performance goals should be achievable but not too easily – account should be taken of any constraints that may affect the individual's capacity to achieve the goals; these could include lack of resources (money, time, equipment, support from other people), lack of experience or training, external factors beyond the individual's control.
- *Agreed* by the manager and the individual concerned – the aim is to provide for the ownership, not the imposition, of goals, although there will be occasions where individuals have to be persuaded to accept a higher standard than they believe themselves to be capable of attaining and individual goals must be consistent with over-arching corporate goals.
- *Time-related*: the timescale or date for reaching targets should be specified.

These are demanding requirements and it is hardly surprising that managers often find it hard to satisfy them.

Setting performance objectives

Conceptually, the basis for performance objective goal setting is provided by definitions of key result areas that are incorporated into a role profile that spells out expected outcomes. When agreeing objectives it is necessary to ask the question: 'How will we know that this goal has been achieved?' The answer is given by a key performance indicator, which defines how information on what has happened will be obtained. Key performance indicators can be established for each key result area and these inform definitions of performance targets and standards.

The overall process

The aim will be to reach agreement on a set of objectives that meet the criteria for an effective goal, listed earlier. Employees should participate fully in the process. This is important because it means that they are more likely to understand and accept what they are expected to do and are therefore more likely to do it. It will be particularly necessary to ensure that the discussion leads to a better understanding of organizational goals and how employees can help to translate them into action with support from the organization and their managers.

Objective setting may start from a clean sheet, but it often doesn't. Objectives may already exist but they may need to be modified to meet the rapidly changing circumstances typical in enterprises these days. This may happen at any time during the year, which is why objective setting cannot be left to an annual performance review meeting.

Managers should explain to individuals how their performance in achieving goals will be monitored and reviewed. It is important for the latter to know that there will be a fair and just process of measurement and assessment and that they will receive feedback on how they are doing. Guidance should also be given to individuals on how they can monitor their own performance by reference to key performance indicators.

The conceptual approaches to defining key result areas, key performance indicators, performance targets and performance standards, are described below. However, in practice it may be best to simplify the process and avoid the use of these jargon terms as much as possible.

Key result areas

Key result areas or KRAs are the elements or core tasks of a role for which clear outputs or outcomes can be defined, each of which makes a significant contribution to achieving the overall purpose of the role. An output is a result that can be measured quantifiably, while an outcome is a visible effect that is the result of effort but cannot necessarily be measured in quantified terms. There are components in all jobs that are difficult to measure quantifiably as outputs, but all jobs produce outcomes even if they are not quantified. As described by Shields (2007): 'In essence a KRA is a significant, distinct area of work activity or accountability, the achievement of which determines or indicates performance effectiveness or success.' A key result area may be described as an accountability – an aspect of the role for which the role holder is responsible (held to account for).

To achieve strategic alignment, the key result areas for a role should so far as possible take account of the key result areas and strategic goals of the organization. There are typically around five to six KRAs in a role. These should cover the range of important tasks that the role holder is expected to perform. For example, the key result areas for a quality control technician could be:

1 Conduct tests to establish the extent to which a range of food products meets quality standards.

2 Monitor the achievement of food hygiene standards and conduct tests to establish the extent to which company and national/international standards are being achieved for the range of products.

3 Recommend actions to remedy quality or hygiene problems identified by the tests.

4 Prepare replies for customer services to send to customers who have complained about the quality of any item in the product range.

5 Prepare regular reports summarizing test results and findings.

6 Contribute to reviews of how quality and hygiene standards can be improved.

The following are other examples of KRA definitions:

- Test new systems to ensure they meet agreed systems specifications.
- Post cash to the nominal and sales ledgers to provide up-to-date and accurate financial information.

- Dispatch the warehouse planned output so that all items are removed by carriers on the same day they are packed.

- Ensure that management accounts are produced that provide the required level of information to management and individual managers on financial performance against budget and on any variances.

- Prepare marketing plans that provide clear guidance on the actions to be taken by the production, marketing and sales departments.

- Plan and implement sales campaigns to meet sales targets.

A KRA definition should be expressed in one sentence starting with an active verb. The content of the KRA definition should focus on the specific purpose of the activity rather than describing in detail the duties involved. Defining too many KRAs will be confusing and make it more difficult to plan, measure and control. The aim should be to focus on the five or six aspects of the job that really matter.

To assist with strategic alignment, managers should start by sharing with the individual the over-arching goals of the organization and the specific goals of their function or department. The relationship between these goals and those of the individual can then be discussed with an emphasis on establishing how the individual can support their achievement.

KRAs as defined in a role profile may be on-going to a certain degree but requirements change and role profiles need to be reviewed regularly and, when necessary, modified. This can take place at any time, but at the planning stage of the performance management cycle it is useful to review the role profile and the associated KRAs to ensure that they are up to date.

Performance targets

Performance targets define the quantifiable results to be attained in a key result area by a defined date or over a period of time. For example:

- Increase market share for product A by x per cent by end of financial year.

- Reduce waiting lists by y per cent within six months.

Targets can also be on-going quantified performance requirements, for example:

- Distribute management accounts to managers within three working days of the end of the accounting period.

- Respond satisfactorily to 90 per cent of customer queries or complaints within 24 hours – the rest to be acknowledged within 24 hours and answered within three working days.

Performance standards

A performance standard is defined in the form of a statement that performance will be up to standard if a specified result happens. The results expected can be defined in such terms as:

- The achievement of already defined operational norms related to administrative procedures, quality and continuous improvement requirements, customer or client satisfaction, levels of service to internal and external customers or good employment practices.

- The ability to meet deadlines.

- The extent to which backlogs are controlled.

- Speed of activity or response to requests.

- Change in the behaviour of employees, customers, clients and other people of importance to the organization.

- The reactions of clients, customers (internal and external) and outside bodies to the service provided.

- The degree to which behaviour supports core values in such areas as quality, care for people and team working.

Here are two examples of performance standards:

- Performance will be up to standard when line managers obtain guidance on inventory control practice that makes a significant contribution to the achievement of inventory targets.

- Performance will be up to standard when proposals for new product development are fully supported by data provided from market research and product-testing programmes.

Key performance indicators

To provide the basis for setting goals and monitoring and reviewing performance it is helpful to answer the question for each key
result area and its associated objective: 'How will we know when the
results specified in this area have been achieved?' The answer to this
question is known as a key performance indicator (KPI). A KPI may
be a metric – a measure providing data that indicate in quantitative
terms the outcome of an activity, for example, performance in terms
of sales value, output (units produced), throughput (units processed),
productivity, cost per unit of output, the volume of such things as
customer complaints, defective components (rejects) or waste, or the
speed with which orders are processed or enquiries dealt with.

Where the use of metrics is not possible it will be necessary to use
a qualitative KPI in the form of a statement that defines the conditions that exist when a job has been well done. The KPIs for the role
of plant manager could be:

- Production output and throughput records.
- Records of productivity in terms of output per person and costs in
  terms of cost per unit of output.
- Information showing that production schedules and plans are real-
  istic and implemented effectively.
- Quality control reports showing results against standards and
  targets.
- Safety records showing frequency rate of accidents.
- Results of employee engagement surveys.

The objective setting sequence

To summarize, the conceptual approach to objective setting involves
three stages:

1 The definition of a role profile containing defined key result areas.
2 The definition of objectives for each key result area.
3 The definition of key performance indicators for each objective.

Figure 6.1   The objective-setting sequence

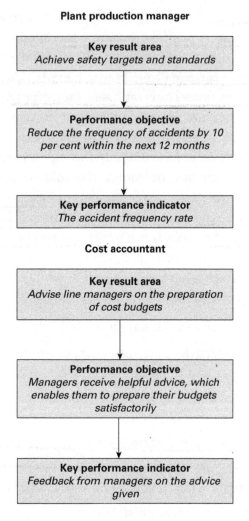

Plant production manager

Key result area
Achieve safety targets and standards

Performance objective
*Reduce the frequency of accidents by 10
per cent within the next 12 months*

Key performance indicator
The accident frequency rate

Cost accountant

Key result area
*Advise line managers on the preparation
of cost budgets*

Performance objective
*Managers receive helpful advice, which
enables them to prepare their budgets
satisfactorily*

Key performance indicator
*Feedback from managers on the advice
given*

Examples of this sequence for a plant production manager (a target) and a cost accountant (a performance standard) are shown in Figure 6.1.

Objective-setting issues

The process of objective setting as just described seems to be logical and easily put into practice. However, there are number of issues, as discussed below.

Complexity

The biggest problem is that the conceptual approach to objective setting may be too complicated and jargon-ridden for the managers and individuals who use the system. It is easy to grasp the notion that it is a good idea for people to know where they are expected to go because if this isn't done, how will they ever get there. They can be encouraged and even taught how to do this as long as they are not overwhelmed with jargon or bothered by elaborate methods. It may, however, be useful in a training session to clarify meaning by using explicit terms such as role profile and key result area.

To simplify the process it would be better to get managers to focus on the basic process of agreeing expectations – what an employee is there to do and how he or she will know that these expectations have been met. It is not essential to worry about defining key performance indicators as a separate activity. In practice, they often find it difficult to distinguish between objectives and performance indicators especially when an objective is defined as a performance standard that may contain an indication of how it will be measured.

The reasons for objective setting and methods of doing it need to be presented to them as the basic performance management process in a much more straightforward way. The explanation would stress that setting objectives is a natural process of management – all managers do it. The approach better managers adopt is to discuss the following questions, the answers to which will in effect produce a role profile and a set of objectives:

1 What is the overall purpose of your job – why does it exist?

2 What are the key things you have to do to achieve that purpose? Try to limit these to five or six activities.

3 For each of these key activities, what are you expected to achieve and how will you know that they have been achieved?

It is best to commit the answers to paper for future reference to cover reviewing performance and establishing development needs. An elaborate form is not necessary.

This approach could be described as taking the mystique out of performance management. Some managers will adopt it because they are good managers; others will need more help. Even the good managers will benefit from some guidance so as to structure their instinctive methods. When considering how to reinvent objective setting along these lines it is useful to think about how it is to be implemented and this means looking at ways of communicating what is involved, training managers in how to do it (especially prospective and new managers) and providing guidance and coaching to existing managers, supplemented where necessary by formal training. Methods of training generally are described in Chapter 10.

Over-emphasis on quantification

Many writers on performance management and many practitioners believe that objectives have to be quantified, but what gets measured in quantified terms is often what is easy to measure. It was observed by Levinson (1970) that: 'The greater the emphasis on measurement and quantification, the more likely the subtle, non-measurable elements of the task will be sacrificed. Quality of performance frequently, therefore, loses out to quantification.'

An over-emphasis on quantification was one of the reasons for the downfall of management by objectives in its original form (the other was over-complexity in the form of too much paperwork). The pursuit of quantification at all costs means that unrealistic targets are set. As Levinson pointed out, it also means that the qualitative aspects of performance that are so important in many jobs are neglected.

The answer to this problem is to set targets wherever they are clear, measurable and appropriate – they are a vital aspect of many jobs – but do not forget the qualitative aspects. Remember that in some jobs and for some tasks within a job, the most relevant objectives are those that describe clearly the circumstances in which it can be established that a job or a task has been performed well, without any spurious figures being attached.

Obsession with SMART objectives

'SMART' as a mnemonic for a desirable objective (described earlier in this chapter) is all the rage. Because it is fashionable and deceptively simple, organizations use it rigidly and without thinking. It was attacked by Chamberlin (2011) but he missed the point. He was unhappy about some of the components of SMART but the real problem is that it is mechanistic and leads to superficial judgements. It also encourages quantification for quantification's sake.

Line managers and individual employees do indeed require some guidance on setting objectives but not in this simplistic form (this is an isolated case of traditional performance management prescriptions erring on the side of over-simplicity rather than over-complexity). The answer is not to provide managers with an easy but facile solution but to get them to focus on the five key requirements of a good objective, namely that it should be:

1 Clear.

2 Challenging.

3 Achievable but not too easy.

4 Measurable either in quantified or in qualitative terms.

5 Agreed.

Aligning individual and organizational objectives

Everyone who writes or talks about performance management refers to the importance of alignment but they seldom mention the practical difficulties of achieving it. Assuming that defined strategic objectives exist and are communicated to those concerned with setting objectives (a big assumption), the basic problem is that of translating generalized strategic goals into specific ones for individuals. It is hard to link a broad corporate goal of, say, increasing market share by x per cent, into goals relating to any key results area of a junior employee such as a data administrator. A corporate strategic goal may refer to specific improvements in performance in an area such as productivity. However, for people who are concerned with production or service delivery, productivity goals will be set or at least should be set whether or not they exist at a strategic level. The strategic alignment of individual objectives is indeed important for anyone who is closely involved in achieving corporate strategic goals and who is concerned with setting the goals of subordinates, but the further people are away from the coal face the more difficult it is to achieve close alignment. This does not mean that it should not be attempted, but there are limitations to the extent to which it can be applied rigorously throughout an organization.

Developing objective-setting skills

Some managers are good at setting objectives, others aren't. Even good managers can benefit from some training and it is absolutely essential for the weaker ones and for those on management development programmes.

An alternative to objectives

The objections to objective setting raised earlier can be alleviated by simplification, training and guidance, but it often remains a difficult concept for employees to grasp. The alternative is to think the unthinkable and abolish the traditional method of setting objectives altogether. This is what Microsoft has done. Instead of setting 'SMART' objectives, employees are expected to maintain a list of their core priorities. These just describe what an individual is going to do, what the expected impact is and any ways to measure or quantify success. An employee's core priorities might be relevant for three weeks, while another priority may be relevant for three years – or anywhere in between. Microsoft guides people to only have between three and five active priorities at a time and suggests that they only need to be two or three sentences long. But how people define their core priorities is very flexible. It is at the control of the employee – although managers' implicit agreement is still required.

This is an approach people may find easier to grasp. They simply have to look at their job and think about the most important things they are expected to do without having to dream up artificial targets and standards for everything. In one job a priority may be to complete a major project. In another, it may be to achieve an agreed sales target. In yet another, it may simply be to regularly carry out the required administrative tasks efficiently and effectively. There is much to be said for this approach.

Conclusions

Setting objectives or goals as the basis for defining the results people should achieve and therefore the direction they should take is a fundamental performance management activity. But there are four issues that affect objective setting:

1 An over-complex objective-setting process.

2 Obsession with SMART objectives.

3 Over-emphasis on quantitative objectives neglecting the fact that in many jobs qualitative objectives are also important.

4 Difficulties in aligning individual and organizational objectives.

These difficulties can be alleviated but are hard to overcome. Perhaps asking people to define priorities rather than set goals would be better.

References

Chamberlin, J (2011) Who put the 'art' in SMART goals? *Management Services*, Autumn, pp 22–27

Latham, G and Locke, R (1979) Goal setting – a motivational technique that works, *Organizational Dynamics*, Autumn, pp 68–80

Latham, G and Locke, E A (2006) Enhancing the benefits and avoiding the pitfalls of goal setting, *Organizational Dynamics*, 35 (4), pp 332–40

Lawler, E E, Benson, G S and McDermott, M (2012) What makes performance appraisals effective? *Compensation & Benefits Review*, 44 (4), pp 191–200

Levinson, H (1970) Management by whose goals? *Harvard Business Review*, July–August, pp 125–34

Locke, R and Latham, G (2004) What should we do about motivation theory? Six recommendations for the twenty-first century, *Academy of Management Review*, **29** (3), pp 398–403

Shields, J (2007) *Managing Employee Performance and Reward*, Cambridge University Press, Port Melbourne

Replace the annual performance review

07

Introduction: performance reviews under attack

The formal performance management review was described succinctly and damningly some time ago by Helen Murlis as a 'dishonest annual ritual'. It has been subject to much more criticism lately. Here are three examples:

> It [performance management] is surely the very bluntest of all the very blunt tools in the HR toolbox. Yet, each year, we drag ourselves through the soul-destroying ritualistic charade that is the annual performance appraisal. This is not thoughtful or considered performance management. Let's just not do it.
>
> (Briner, 2012)

> The yearly review causes such dread. Should we kill it? Annual reviews often discourage employees rather than motivating them.
>
> (HR Magazine, 2012)

In many organizations, the performance appraisal has degenerated into a mere formality, and a fruitless one at that. Employers and employees are jointly complicit, dutifully sitting across from one another but simply going through the motions, ticking off goals and targets achieved over the past 12 months, those that weren't, and a new set of goals and targets for the next 12 months. As performance management tools, these by-the-numbers appraisals don't hold much value for most companies, and they do little to raise employee engagement, commitment or satisfaction levels.

(Reviewsnap, 2015)

This chapter begins with a description of the traditional approach to performance reviews or appraisals and the flaws that have prompted the adverse comments. It then refers to examples of responses to the attacks, which is followed by an explanation of how to make the performance reviewing process more effective.

The traditional approach to performance reviews

The traditional approach to performance reviews or appraisals (the terms are interchangeable) is for managers to meet individual members of their team to assess performance. The most common practice is to have one annual review, as carried out by 65 per cent of respondents to the survey conducted by Armstrong and Baron (2005). Twice-yearly reviews were held by 27 per cent of the respondents.

Purposes

The purposes the review is supposed to serve are:

- *assessment* – to review how well individuals have performed their jobs;
- *objective setting* – to set new objectives and revise existing ones;
- *development planning* – to agree performance and personal development plans;
- *motivation* – to provide positive feedback and recognition;
- *communication* – to serve as a two-way channel for communication about roles, expectations, relationships, work problems and aspirations;
- *reward* – to assess performance in order to inform reward decisions, especially those concerning performance pay;

- *talent management* – to identify potential as part of a talent management programme;
- *poor performance* – to establish what action is needed to deal with an under-performer.

Method

Formal reviews include an overview and analysis of performance since the last review, comparing results with agreed expectations and plans. In a sense, they are supposed to be stocktaking exercises. Ideally, reference is made to events that illustrate performance as discussed during the year (they shouldn't be brought up at a formal meeting for the first time). The level of performance achieved is assessed so that individuals know where they stand. In many cases it is rated. Formal reviews are usually documented on paper or recorded on a computer.

How the ideal review should be conducted

There are 12 'golden' rules' for conducting an ideal formal performance review meeting:

1 *Be prepared*. Managers should prepare by referring to a list of agreed goals and their notes on performance throughout the year. They should form views about the reasons for success or failure and decide where to give praise, which performance problems should be mentioned and what steps might be undertaken to overcome them. Thought should also be given to any changes that have taken place or are contemplated in the individual's role and to work and personal objectives for the next period. Individuals should also prepare in order to identify achievements and problems, and to be ready to assess their own performance at the meeting. They should also note any points they wish to raise about their work and prospects.

2 *Work to a clear structure*. The meeting should be planned to cover all the points identified during preparation. Sufficient time should be allowed for a full discussion – hurried meetings will be

ineffective. An hour or two is usually necessary to get maximum value from the review.

3   *Create the right atmosphere.* A successful meeting depends on creating an informal environment in which a full, frank but friendly exchange of views can take place. It is best to start with a fairly general discussion that aims to put the individual at ease and create a non-threatening atmosphere and which covers the purpose of the meeting, emphasizing that it is a joint affair before getting into any detail.

4   *Provide good feedback.* Individuals need to know how they are getting on. Feedback needs to be based on factual evidence and careful thought should be given to what is said and how it is said so that it motivates rather than demotivates people.

5   *Use time productively.* The reviewer should test understanding, obtain information, and seek proposals and support. Time should be allowed for the individual to express his or her views fully and to respond to any comments made by the manager. The meeting should take the form of a dialogue between two interested and involved parties, both of whom are seeking a positive conclusion.

6   *Use praise.* If possible, managers should begin with praise for some specific achievement, but this should be sincere and deserved. Praise helps people to relax – everyone needs encouragement and appreciation.

7   *Let individuals do most of the talking.* This enables them to get things off their chest and helps them to feel that they are getting a fair hearing. Use open-ended questions (ie questions that invite the individual to think about what to reply rather than indicating the expected answer). This is to encourage people to expand.

8   *Invite self-assessment.* This is to see how things look from the individual's point of view and to provide a basis for discussion – many people underestimate themselves.

9   *Discuss performance not personality.* Discussions on performance should be based on factual evidence, not opinion. Always refer to actual events or behaviour and to results compared with agreed performance measures. Individuals should be given plenty of scope to explain why something did or did not happen.

10 *Encourage analysis of performance.* Don't just hand out praise or blame. Analyse jointly and objectively why things went well or badly and what can be done to maintain a high standard or avoid problems in the future.

11 *Don't deliver unexpected criticisms.* There should be no surprises. The discussion should only be concerned with events or behaviours that have been noted at the time they took place. Feedback on performance should be immediate: it should not wait until the end of the year. The purpose of the formal review is to reflect briefly on experiences during the review period and on this basis to look ahead.

12 *Agree measurable objectives and a plan of action.* The aim should be to end the review meeting on a positive note.

Problems with formal performance reviews

The fundamental problem is that getting managers to conduct a performance review once a year creates the impression that the management of someone's performance can be accomplished in the hour or so that it takes to complete the review. What happens during the rest of the year does not matter. A yearly meeting means that insufficient attention may be given to what happened some time ago and assessments will be subjected to the 'recency' effect, ie focusing on recent events rather than looking at the whole picture. Furthermore, waiting for 12 months before setting new objectives is unrealistic in today's fast-moving conditions. Taking part in a traditional formal performance review can be a daunting and therefore dreaded occasion for both parties. Conducting satisfactory reviews requires considerable skill. The 12 requirements for a successful meeting are demanding.

Then there is the multiplicity of purposes. How can all of them be satisfied in one brief meeting? It is impossible. As long ago as 1998 a manager in a financial services company commented to Armstrong and Baron (1998) that there was a culture of 'cram it all into one meeting'. More recently, Lisa Dodge, Director, Global Performance Programmes at Microsoft, said that its previous approach tried to do too many things:

It was like a Swiss army knife of performance management – we were using it for everything from allocating reward to categorizing talent. The ratings people received became an overarching label of everything anyone in the company felt they needed to know about someone. And it became a gate to things – whether or not an employee could transfer, for example, or even whether or not they should transfer. It wasn't intentional, but it happened. And our employees didn't like it – which worked against the programme's ability to help improve performance.

That many managers and, indeed, employees generally find it difficult is hardly surprising. They cannot be blamed for paying lip-service to something they cannot comprehend and find daunting and just about impossible to do well. As a result meetings can be superficial, inconclusive and even demotivating. It can only work if the purposes are simplified and there is mutual trust and understanding between the perceptions of both parties; without this, hostility and resistance are likely to emerge.

The golden rules set out above may sound straightforward and obvious enough but they will only function properly in a culture that supports this type of approach. This is why it is essential to get and keep top management support and to take special care in developing and introducing the system and in training managers *and* their staff. It is also necessary to remember that reinventing performance management is not something that can be done overnight. It will take time, effort and persistence.

How are organizations responding to the challenge and the problems?

In response to the attacks and problems referred to above, the annual performance review is the part of performance management that has been most subject to reinvention. As reported by Justine Hofherr (2015):

The NeuroLeadership Institute is a global research organization that specializes in studying neuroscience and leadership. It looked at 33 of the 52 companies who had moved from the process of annual performance reviews to more unconventional ways of performance management by November 2015.

Researchers found that by and large, organizations saw a range of positive outcomes from the shift which included better communication between managers and employees, reduced administrative burden and a greater focus on employee growth and development.

More frequent interactions had such a positive response that more than 50 per cent of the organizations studied incorporated them into their new performance analyses. 76 per cent of the 33 companies recommended an annual performance conversation before moving away from performance ratings. However, after the change, 68 per cent recommended conversations once a quarter as a minimum.

The study by the NeuroLeadership Institute also found that killing performance reviews significantly reduced administrative burden, with nearly two-thirds of the 33 organizations reducing managers' documentation requirements for performance conversations with workers. This translated into huge savings in terms of time and money. For example, Deloitte had been spending nearly two million hours annually to review over 65,000 employees around the world.

Here are some examples of what companies have been doing about annual reviews.

Adobe

The annual review meeting has been replaced by manager and employee 'check-ins' covering expectations, feedback, growth and development agenda, to be whenever sensible but at least quarterly.

Accenture

As reported by the *Washington Post* (2015), Pierre Nanterne, the CEO of Accenture, commented that:

We're done with the famous annual performance review, where once a year I'm going to share with you what I think about you. That doesn't make any sense. Performance is an on-going activity. It's every day, after any client interaction or business interaction or corporate interaction.

It's much more fluid. People want to know on an on-going basis, am I doing right? Am I moving in the right direction? Do you think I'm progressing? Nobody's going to wait for an annual cycle to get that feedback. Now it's all about instant performance management.

Deloitte

Deloitte replaced the formal annual review with regular 'check-ins' conducted by team leaders with each team member about current work. These conversations allow leaders to set expectations, review priorities, comment on recent work, and provide correction, coaching and important new information.

Gap Inc

The new approach to performance management at Gap Inc is called 'Grow. Perform. Succeed.' (Its abbreviation, GPS, is also the company's stock symbol.) By redesigning its performance management system and giving it a new name, the company repositioned the process as less of a threat, an important step to better conversations.

The change involved the introduction of 12 'touch base' sessions to replace the single year-end review meeting. These are intended to be informal discussions between managers and employees that can take place anywhere and at any time. None of these conversations is recorded.

The meetings may be used to discuss any aspect of performance, although ideally employees should revisit their objectives to make sure they are still relevant and to see if there are any new ones that need to be added or current ones that need to be taken away. Their performance is against the new performance standard. Are they learning from their successes and failure? Are they demonstrating the values of the company? The discussion may cover key working relationships and career aspirations. It is intended to focus on these larger topics, rather than the day-to-day aspects of work.

The existing Gap feedback model is used, which encourages managers to ask employees three questions:

1 What went well?

2 Where did you get stuck?

3 What would you do differently next time?

The belief is that using this simple model facilitates a real two-way conversation rather than just forcing the employee to listen to what the manager has to say.

IBM

A new app-based performance review system called 'Checkpoint' has been introduced. This enables employees to set shorter-term goals, and managers will provide feedback on their progress at least every quarter.

Microsoft

The formal annual performance review has been replaced by what are called 'Connects'. These are regular conversations between managers and employees. Every employee is expected to have a minimum of two Connects a year; beyond this, Microsoft does not apply any strict rules.

To ensure managers and employees get the most out of their Connects, Microsoft developed a simple framework to help structure the conversations. Each Connect is centred on four questions, two of which look back and two of which look forward.

The two questions that look back at the employee's performance are: What impact did you have, and what opportunities were there for greater impact? The two questions designed to help the employees look forward are: What are your upcoming deliverables, and what will you do to learn and grow in the upcoming period?

Along with these questions, employees are also expected to maintain a list of their core priorities. They are the overarching goals that people are trying to achieve. How people define their core priorities is very flexible. It is in the control of the employee – although managers' implicit agreement is still required.

Tasty Catering

At Chicago's Tasty Catering, performance appraisals are no longer a once-a-year event. Instead, managers and employees meet every three months to discuss what's on their minds. Employees have to answer just two questions: What do you want to do differently? What are your personal wants?

Union Bank & Trust

The new 'Four by Four' performance review process at Union Bank & Trust requires managers to meet with direct reports four times a year at regularly scheduled intervals. However, there are no ratings – no numbers or terminology that attempt to sum up an employee's performance. Instead, managers hold conversations with their people, asking them four key questions:

1 What have you accomplished in the last six months?

2 What will you accomplish in the next six months?

3 What challenges are you facing?

4 How can I help you be your best?

Texas Roadhouse

Texas Roadhouse calls its new process 'GPS' (Growth, Plan and Support). Its purpose is to be forward-looking instead of backward. The company's performance appraisals now focus on just three issues: 1) career opportunities employees would like in the future; 2) how employees will prepare for these future opportunities; and 3) the resources employees need to be successful. The review process has also been decoupled from merit increases.

Reinventing the performance review

For all the reasons given earlier it is clear that the annual or half-yearly performance review is dead. It must be replaced by a process that recognizes what should be obvious – that managing performance is something that happens throughout the year, not just at infrequent intervals. This is what the organizations listed above are doing and it is what anyone who wants a performance management system that works must do.

So what's to be done? The answer is to replace the annual review with more frequent meetings that are given various names such as 'check-ins', 'connects', 'touch base meetings', or 'performance and development conversations (PDCs)'. The name is a matter of choice but 'PDC' conveys the essence of what takes place and is used in this book. PDCs can take place at least four times a year or, better still, even more frequently as and when appropriate. At Deloitte it was established that the best way to ensure frequency was to have what they call check-ins initiated by the team member – who more often than not is eager for the guidance and attention they provide – rather than by the team leader.

As the term indicates, PDCs take the form of a conversation rather than a formal review. They include feedback from the manager and, possibly, some self-assessment by the individual. They are rooted in the reality of what the individual is doing. PDCs are concrete not abstract. They focus on the goals people set for themselves and how they are progressing toward those goals, along with their contribution, past and present, to the company. They focus on strengths rather than dwelling on shortcomings. Successes are recognized although things that have not gone according to plan will be noted in order to learn lessons for the future. They do not lead to a performance rating or the completion of a report, although a note can be taken of any agreed actions.

Importantly, PDCs provide a means of identifying and addressing personal development needs and therefore for encouraging continuous development, as discussed in Chapter 9. They also provide opportunities for revising or renewing objectives and development plans. Reference may be made to recent events but the emphasis is on the future. They are not post-mortems. As Colbert (2010) proposed, they should be *previews* not *reviews*.

David Rock (Rock *et al*, 2014) noted that:

One key element is to prime people – both the employee and the boss – to induce a growth mind-set. This improves how people listen to feedback, encourages them to set stretch goals, makes it easier for them to put in extra effort toward a worthy project, and helps them learn from positive role models.

Although their simplified format does not demand the excessively wide range of skills needed by the traditional annual review, skills are still required to conduct a PDC, especially those concerned with providing feedback and handling the challenging conversations that may occur when the feedback is negative.

Conclusions

The annual performance review or appraisal has been subject to much criticism lately. The fundamental problem is that getting managers to conduct a performance review once a year creates the impression that the management of someone's performance can be accomplished in the hour or so that it takes to conduct what can easily be an unsatisfactory experience for both parties. What happens during the rest of the year does not matter. Even when the less common practice of two meetings a year is adopted the gap between meetings is too wide. A yearly meeting means that insufficient attention may be given to what happened some time ago and assessments will be subjected to the 'recency' effect, ie focusing on recent events rather than looking at the whole picture. Furthermore, waiting for 12 months before setting new objectives is unrealistic in today's fast-moving conditions.

Taking part in a traditional formal performance review can be a daunting and therefore dreaded occasion for both parties. Conducting satisfactory reviews requires considerable skill: the 12 requirements for a successful meeting are demanding. Then there is the multiplicity of purposes. How can all of them be satisfied in one brief meeting? It is impossible. That many managers and, indeed, employees generally find it difficult is hardly surprising. They cannot be blamed for paying lip-service to something they cannot comprehend, find daunting and just about impossible to do well. As a result meetings can be superficial, inconclusive and even demotivating. It can only work if the purposes are simplified and there is mutual trust and understanding between both parties; otherwise hostility and resistance are likely to emerge.

Traditional performance reviews should be replaced by a process that recognizes what should be obvious – that managing performance is something that happens throughout the year, not just at infrequent intervals. The annual performance review can be substituted by less formal performance and development conversations (PDCs). They include feedback from the manager and, possibly, some self-assessment by the individual. They focus on the goals or priorities people set for themselves, how they are progressing toward those goals and their development needs.

References

Armstrong, M and Baron, A (1998) *Performance Management: The new realities*, CIPD, London

Armstrong, M and Baron, A (2005) *Managing Performance: Performance management in action*, CIPD, London

Briner, R (2012) http://www.hrmagazine.co.uk/article-details/whats-the-evidence-for-performance-management (accessed 31 March 2016)

Colbert, S A (2010) *Get Rid of the Performance Review*, Hachette, New York

Hofherr, J (2015) What really happens when companies kill performance reviews, Boston.com, https://www.boston.com/jobs/jobs-news/2015/11/17/what-really-happens-when-companies-kill-performance-reviews (accessed 9 April 2016)

HR Magazine (2012) http://www.hrmagazine.co.uk/article-details/is-it-time-to-give-up-on-performance-appraisals (accessed 31 March 2016)

Reviewsnap (2015) http://www.reviewsnap.com/documents/white_papers/Reviewsnap_The Truth_About_Performance_Appraisals.pdf (accessed 31 March 2016)

Rock, D, Davis, J and Jones, B (2014) *Kill Your Performance Ratings*, Strategy+Business, www.strategy-business.com/article/00275?gko=c442b (accessed 30 March 2016)

Washington Post (2015) https://www.washingtonpost.com/news/on-leadership/wp/2015/07/23/accenture-ceo-explains-the-reasons-why-hes-overhauling-performance-reviews/ (accessed 31 March 2016)

Abolish rating 08

Introduction

Rating involves an assessment by a reviewer of the level of performance of an employee expressed on a scale. The e-reward survey (2014) of performance management found that 77 per cent of respondents used ratings. Since the days of merit rating and then performance appraisal, rating still reigns supreme. To many people it was and is the ultimate purpose and the final outcome of performance appraisal. Academics, especially American academics, have been preoccupied with rating – what it is, how to do it, how to improve it, how to train raters – for the last 50 years. They have identified many problems with rating but it doesn't seem to have occurred to them that these could readily be overcome if rating wasn't used at all.

An approach that is particularly common in the United States is forced ranking. A forced ranking system involves placing employees in rank order according to an assessment of their performance and then dividing the rank order into percentiles, eg the top 20 per cent, the middle 70 per cent and the bottom 10 per cent. The aim is to put employees into categories such as high flyers (the top 20 per cent in this example), unacceptable (the bottom 10 per cent) or those performing at an acceptable but not exceptional level (the remaining 70 per cent). This classification can be used to identify those who are fast-tracked in talent management programmes, or those who may not survive in the organization. The distribution of performance rankings between the different groups is sometimes called a 'vitality curve'. The term 'forced ranking' is a bit of a misnomer. It implies that the rank order is enforced, which is not the case. The only forced provision in such a system is that the division of the rank order into different categories or percentiles is predetermined and everyone concerned has to be forced into one of those categories.

An associated approach is a forced distribution system. This does not involve ranking but does require managers to conform to a laid down distribution of performance ratings, for example the highest level performers would be placed in category A, the middle 70 per cent would have to be placed in category B and the remaining 15 per cent would be placed in category C.

The issue of whether or not to have ratings is much more controversial than the problems raised by annual performance reviews. Organizations that gladly abolish annual reviews are reluctant to give up rating, although they sometimes abandon forced ranking or forced distribution because of the objections to them referred to in Chapter 5.

This chapter starts with analyses of the cases for and against ranking and goes on to reach conclusions on what can be done in a reinvention programme, including the use of alternative methods of performance assessment. It then covers forced ranking and is completed with discussions of what can be done with the processes of deciding on performance pay increases and identifying those with potential for promotion in the absence of ratings.

Rating

Performance rating scales summarize the level of performance achieved by an employee. This is done by selecting the point on a scale (sometimes referred to as a 'performance anchor') that most closely corresponds with the view of the assessor on how well the individual has been doing. A rating scale is supposed to assist in making judgements and it enables those judgements to be categorized to summarize the assessment of overall performance.

Types of scales

Overall rating scales can be defined alphabetically (A, B, C, etc), or numerically (1, 2, 3, etc). The e-reward survey (2014) found that the most popular number of levels was five (61 per cent of respondents). A typical five-point scale looks like this:

A Outstanding performance in all respects.

B Superior performance, significantly above normal job requirements.

C Good all round performance that meets the normal requirements of the job.

D Performance not fully up to requirements. Clear weaknesses requiring improvement have been identified.

E Unacceptable; constant guidance is required and performance of many aspects of the job is well below a reasonable standard.

The theory of rating

The theory underpinning all rating methods is that it is possible as well as desirable to measure the performance of people on a scale accurately and consistently, and categorize them accordingly. As DeNisi and Pritchard (2006) commented: 'Effective performance appraisal systems are those where the raters have the ability to measure employee performance and the motivation to assign the most accurate ratings.'

Murphy and Cleveland (1995) distinguished between judgement and ratings. A judgement is a relatively private evaluation of a person's performance in some area. Ratings are a public statement of a judgement evaluation that is made for the record. Wherry and Bartlett (1982) produced the following theory of the rating process:

- Raters vary in the accuracy of ratings given in direct proportion to the relevancy of their previous contacts with the person being rated.

- Rating items that refer to frequently performed acts are rated more accurately than those which refer to acts performed more rarely.

- The rater makes more accurate ratings when forewarned of the behaviours to be rated because this focuses attention on the particular behaviours.

- Deliberate direction to the behaviours to be assessed reduces rating bias.

- Keeping a written record between rating periods of specifically observed critical incidents improves the accuracy of recall.

Research conducted on rating has produced a number of findings that supplement this theory. Pulakos *et al* (2008) noted that if a system is strictly developmental, there is less need for ratings and in fact they may detract from development. This is because employees tend to be more concerned about their 'score' than their understanding of their development needs. From a development perspective, narratives may provide more useful information than numerical ratings. Even when performance is rated against defined standards the ratings do not convey what the employee did or did not do in sufficient detail. Jawahar and Williams (1997) reported that performance evaluations such as ratings obtained for administrative purposes (eg pay or promotions) are more lenient than those for research, feedback or employee development purposes.

One of the issues concerning assessment is the degree to which receivers accept what the reviewer says about them. Research by Roberts (1994) indicated that acceptance is maximized when the performance measurement process is perceived to be accurate, the system is administered fairly, the assessment system doesn't conflict with the employee's values and when the assessment process does not exceed the bounds of the psychological contract. He suggested that to increase the acceptability of assessments reviewers should:

- Pay less attention to mechanics and place more emphasis on process.

- Avoid basing conclusions on a small number of instances.

- Learn to seek information on external factors that may influence performance.

- Document employee performance.

- Involve individuals in the process through a genuine invitation to participate.

- Appreciate that reviewers do not have all the relevant performance information and that the employee is an important source.

- Encourage self-appraisal.
- Provide regular informal feedback, bearing in mind that once a year performance appraisal is unlikely to meet employee feedback requirements.

Fletcher (2001) reported that many studies have demonstrated that performance ratings become more positive over time, as was confirmed by Silverman *et al* (2005). Rather than indicating performance improvement, this could simply arise because raters become complacent, or careless or both.

Strebler *et al* (2001) commented that: 'The psychometric properties of the rating process – ie whether achieved ratings are valid and a true measure of actual performance – is the most researched aspect of performance assessment.' Their study of a care organization established that people became focused on the review headings (a little like wasps around jam) for the sole purpose of getting points (and points mean prizes) rather than improving the quality of care they delivered. Saffie-Robertson and Brutus (2014) found through their research that evaluators who are uncomfortable about the appraisal process tend to inflate their performance ratings.

Arguments in favour of rating

Those who support rating – the majority – see it as an essential means of summing up performance, informing performance pay decisions, identifying poor performers and defining potential. In more detail, the arguments for rating are that:

- It satisfies a natural wish people have to know where they stand. But this is only desirable if the manager's opinion is honest, justified and fair, and the numbers or letters convey what is really felt and are meaningful.
- It provides a convenient means of summing up judgements so that high or low performances can easily be identified (as long as the judgements are consistent and fair).
- It motivates people by giving people something to strive for in the shape of higher ratings (as long as they know what they have to do to get a better assessment).

- It is not possible to have performance-related pay without an overall rating (but assuming performance pay is wanted or needed there is an alternative approach to decision making; see the penultimate section in this chapter).

- It can provide a basis for identifying high flyers for a talent management programme or for generally predicting potential. But past performance is only a predictor of future performance when there is a connecting link, ie there are elements of the present job that are also important in a higher level job.

Arguments against rating

Ratings are largely subjective and it is difficult to achieve consistency between the ratings given by different managers. Because the notion of 'performance' is often unclear, subjectivity can increase. Even if objectivity is achieved, to sum up the total performance of a person with a single rating is a gross over-simplification of what may be a complex set of factors influencing that performance – to do this suggests that the rating will be a superficial and arbitrary judgement. To label people as 'average' or 'below average', or whatever equivalent terms are used, is both demeaning and demotivating. The whole performance review may be dominated by the fact that it will end with a rating, thus severely limiting the forward-looking and developmental focus of the meeting, which is all-important. This is particularly the case if the rating governs performance pay increases.

Furnham (2004) raised a number of questions about the rating process, including the issue of what should be observed and recorded, the availability of reliable performance standards and the evaluative and judgmental nature of the process.

There are many well-known rating errors. Grote (1996) lists nine:

1 *Contrast effect.* The tendency of a rater to evaluate people in comparison with other individuals rather than against the standards for the job.

2 *First impression error.* The tendency of a manager to make an initial positive or negative judgement of an employee and allow that first impression to colour or distort later information.

3 *Halo or horns effect.* Inappropriate generalizations from one aspect of an individual's performance to all areas of that person's performance.

4 *Similar-to-me effect.* The tendency of individuals to rate people who resemble themselves more highly than they rate others.

5 *Central tendency.* The inclination to rate people in the middle of the scale even when their performance clearly warrants a substantially higher or lower rating.

6 *Negative and positive skew.* The opposite of central tendency: the rating of all individuals as higher or lower than their performance actually warrants.

7 *Attribution bias.* The tendency to attribute performance failings to factors under the control of the individual and performance successes to external causes.

8 *Recency effect.* The tendency of minor events that have happened recently to have more influence on the rating than major events of many months ago.

9 *Stereotyping.* The tendency to generalize across groups and ignore individual differences.

Attacks on rating

Powerful attacks on rating were made by Coens and Jenkins (2002) and Lee (2005).

Coens and Jenkins

- Ratings are not a good idea because of the unintended consequences – the insidious, destructive and counterproductive effects of giving people ratings about their work performance. Whether accurate or not, people are psychologically affected by ratings. And except for people rated at the highest end of the scale, the impact is usually negative... Our ability to fairly measure the performance level of an individual is severely hampered by the unknowable effects of systems and random variations.

Lee

- The rating process is actually a by-product of the attempt to measure performance outcomes. An excessive emphasis on measurement can be misguided. The desired end that is lost in measuring performance is not measurement at all, but rather description.

- Poor ratings can stigmatize performance and cause unnecessary resistance to the acceptance of feedback.

- The goal is to have the employee assist us in describing, interpreting and redirecting performance feedback, not reacting to the ratings. Feedback can accomplish the same positive goal as a rating without the negative side effects.

- If the goal is performance improvement, then feedback – not labelling past efforts – is the preferred tool.

- Although ratings can be positive they can also be punitive and focus attention on the negative rather than the possible. The only message the employee gets from a poor rating is: 'Stop doing what you have been punished for doing.' This kind of rating may not even be an adequate description, since many ratings are a summary of a number of activities collected over time. It does not focus attention on what to do to get better.

- Ratings are feedback but feedback of the worst kind.

David Rock, Director of the NeuroLeadership Institute, told Justine Hofherr (2015):

> People are concerned that organizations won't know how to rate performance or differentiate between pay without them. However, this isn't true. The majority of organizations making the change are giving more discretion to managers to decide who gets a pay rise and who doesn't. They feel that the established numerical ranking system is 'counter-intuitive' to creating employee improvement.

> Although it seems useful and logical to assign a number to employees and identify them with a 1–5 rating, this can have unexpected and unintended consequences. As humans, we focus on social interactions and are preoccupied with our social status. Calling people a number can trigger a sense of danger in people. It's how we're built.

Although some organizations were worried that removing performance reviews would make top performers feel unappreciated, in fact, employees from all different levels of performance said they were happier without the numerical ratings.

Instead of using numbers, these companies encouraged managers to describe employees' performance after getting to know them through regular interactions. This not only led to managers talking more with employees, but also improved the quality of the conversations. Rather than focusing on past performance, employees and their managers reported setting goals, planning development and taking action.

Research by Scullen and Mount (2000) revealed the subjective nature of ratings. Their study – in which 4,492 managers were rated on certain performance dimensions by two bosses, two peers and two subordinates – showed that 62 per cent of the variance in the ratings could be accounted for by individual rater's peculiarities of perception. Actual performance accounted for only 21 per cent of the variance. This led the researchers to conclude that: 'Our results show that a greater proportion of variance in ratings is associated with biases of the rater than with the performance of the ratee.'

Developments in rating

The examples in Chapter 4 illustrated how five organizations – Adobe, Accenture, Deloitte, Gap and Microsoft – have abandoned ratings. In the latter firm, it was established that scrapping ratings reduced the fear and anxiety that employees felt about discussing performance and that people were therefore much happier to take part in the process. Two other cases, reported by Hofherr (2015), are set out below.

Juniper Networks

Steven Rice of Juniper Networks, a multinational corporation based in California that develops and markets networking products, comments that:

An engineer in our Bangalore Excellence Center pointed out that our performance management process was a violation of our values, because the forced ratings didn't enable leaders to authentically provide feedback or truly trust their judgement to administer rewards.

That led Rice to realize that they could not fix the system piecemeal; Juniper had to imagine a whole new kind of practice, one that 'delivers the benefits without the unintended negative consequences'.

Since 2011, Juniper has not given ratings to employees or kept documents of ratings. It also eliminated forced rankings. The new method focuses heavily on regular quality conversations between managers and employees, using the structured conversation model. Overall, Juniper has seen participation and satisfaction skyrocket among employees and managers.

Cargill

Sharon Arad, an HR executive at Cargill, a global company based in Minneapolis that provides food, agriculture and financial and industrial products and services, describes how the company reviewed its performance management system a few years ago:

> We found the system failed to generate quality conversations, leaving employees with a [ranking] that many viewed as a deficiency statement. In the end, the ratings given were not a trustworthy indicator of the actual status of performance or engagement.

Many Cargill leaders wondered whether removing the ratings would bring about more desirable results and better conversations. So they set up a no-rating pilot of several thousand employees for three years. Every year Arad's team compared the pilot group's feedback to that of a random sample of rated employees. 'Overall, 90 per cent of the no-rating pilot participants reported, year after year, that their experience was positive,' Arad says. This was in stark contrast to the feedback that people normally gave about their performance management experience. Cargill adopted the no-rating approach for its entire organization. The results of no-rating systems are dramatically better than their rating and ranking counterparts – in satisfaction, retention and engagement scores, which have been shown to correlate to organizational performance.

Alternatives to rating

The most drastic alternative to rating is to abandon it altogether, as in the two examples above. Performance and development conversations (PDCs) as described in Chapter 7 would focus on the future, setting goals and agreeing development needs and the actions required to satisfy them. It would still be necessary to make performance pay decisions and identify potential but, as discussed at the end of this chapter, these would not be governed by a crude overall rating. If the pros and cons of rating are analysed this seems on balance to be the most reasonable step. However, if this is considered to be too radical, other alternatives are a visual assessment system and the use of a performance commentary, as described below.

Visual assessment

An alternative approach to rating is to use a visual method of assessment. This takes the form of an agreement between the manager and the individual on where the latter should be placed on a matrix or grid, as illustrated in Figure 8.1, which was developed for a charity. A 'snapshot' is thus provided of the individual's overall contribution,

Figure 8.1 A performance matrix

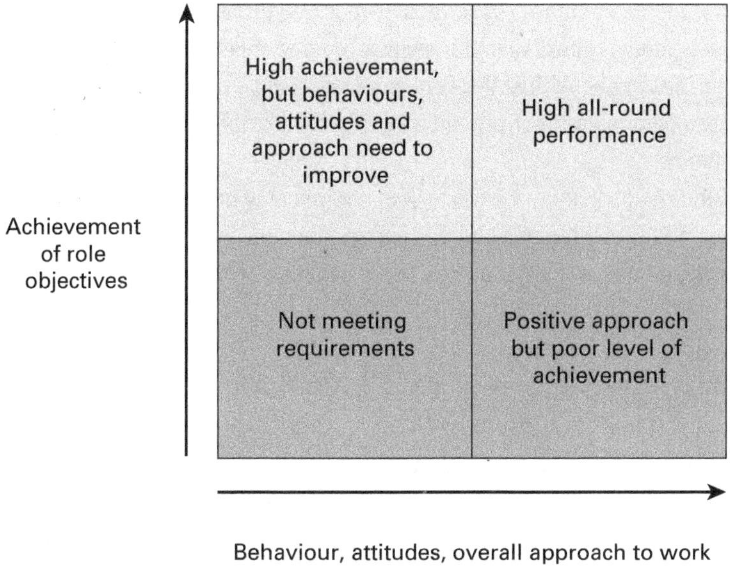

Behaviour, attitudes, overall approach to work

which is presented visually and can thus provide a better basis for analysis and discussion than a mechanistic rating. The assessment of contribution refers both to outputs and to behaviours. The review guidelines accompanying the matrix are shown in the following box.

Review guidelines

You and your manager need to agree an overall assessment. This will be recorded in the summary page at the beginning of the review document. The aim is to get a balanced assessment of your contribution through the year. The assessment will take account of how you have performed against the responsibilities of your role as described in the role profile; objectives achieved and competency development over the course of the year. The assessment will become relevant for pay increases in the future.

The grid on the annual performance review summary is meant to provide a visual snapshot of your overall contribution. This replaces a more conventional rating scale approach. It reflects the fact that your contribution is determined not just by results, but also by your overall approach towards your work and how you behave towards colleagues and customers. The evidence recorded in the performance review will be used to support where your manager places a mark on the grid.

Your manager's assessment against the *vertical axis* will be based on an assessment of your performance against your objectives, performance standards described in your role profile, and any other work achievements recorded in the review. Together these represent 'outputs'. The assessment against the *horizontal axis* will be based on an overall assessment of your performance against the competency level definitions for the role.

Note that someone who is new in the role may be placed in one of the lower quadrants but this should be treated as an indication of development needs and not as a reflection on the individual's performance.

A similar matrix approach has been adopted in a financial services company. It is used for management appraisals to illustrate their performance against peers. It is not an 'appraisal rating': the purpose of the matrix is to help individuals focus on what they do well and on any areas for improvement. Two dimensions – business performance and behaviour (management style) – are reviewed on the matrix, shown

Figure 8.2 Performance matrix in a financial services company

in Figure 8.2, to ensure a rounder discussion of overall contribution against the full role demands rather than a short-term focus on current results. This is achieved by visual means: the individual is placed at the relevant position in the matrix by reference to the two dimensions. For example, a strong people manager who is low on the deliverables would be placed somewhere in the top left-hand quadrant; the aim will be movement to a position in the top right-hand quadrant.

A performance matrix used by a division of Unilever is shown in Figure 8.3. This measures the 'how' of performance on the vertical

Figure 8.3 Assessment and action matrix – Unilever

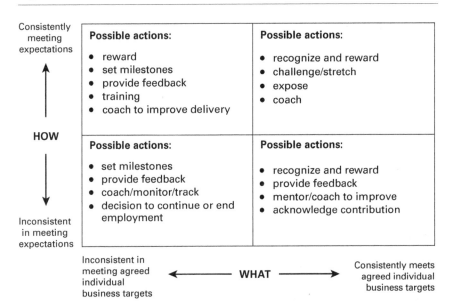

axis and the 'what' on the horizontal axis. The matrix model also contains guidelines on the possible actions that can be taken for each assessment quadrant.

Those organizations that have used visual assessments are enthusiastic about the extent to which it takes the heat out of rating and provides a sound basis for discussing and implementing development needs.

Performance commentary

An overall assessment may be recorded in a narrative, often called a 'performance commentary', consisting of a written summary of views about the level of performance achieved. This method was adopted by 27 per cent of the respondents to the e-reward contingent pay survey (2004). It at least ensures that managers have to collect their thoughts together and put them down on paper.

A performance commentary can summarize the discussions managers and their direct reports have had throughout the year during their regular performance and development conversations or check-ins. It is a reflection of what emerged during these discussions. A commentary is more than simply an assessment: it should demonstrate how managers and their direct reports are working together to manage performance, and how the latter are responding to coaching and feedback.

The following are guidelines on writing a commentary produced by Lloyds Banking Group:

- Get to the point – quantity is no indication of quality when it comes to feedback, so focus efforts on capturing the most important points of feedback, concentrating on outcomes and ensuring that each point is supported by tangible evidence.

- Comment equally on both 'what' has been achieved and 'how' it has been delivered – emphasize both what the individual has done and how he or she has gone about doing it, making explicit reference to the core values of the organization.

- Reflect the dialogue that has occurred throughout the year in what should have been effective and regular performance conversations – it should not be a surprise to the individual concerned.

- Highlight strengths and areas for development – provide acknowledgement of positive contributions, and be constructive in commenting on what the individual might have done differently or to a higher standard.
- Prepare a succinct, results-focused summary.

However, in spite of these guidelines commentaries can be bland, misleading and unhelpful from the viewpoint of deciding what should be done to develop talent or improve performance. If this approach is used, managers should be fully trained in how to do it. An example of a performance commentary is given below.

Performance commentary example

What has been achieved

- Martin has done well in achieving all his performance targets, in fact significantly exceeding two out of the five targets. For example, he overcame a serious setback to reduce his reject rates to the required level.
- He has also generally met the performance standards associated with his role.
- He has made some attempt to implement his development plan but has shown insufficient perseverance in covering some of the broader knowledge-acquisition requirements.

How it has been achieved

- Martin shows initiative and needs relatively little guidance or supervision. He leads his team well. His contribution to supporting the core values of the organization, especially those concerned with care for quality and care for individuals, is admirable. For example, he has successfully introduced an entirely new quality control system. And he pays a lot of attention to his coaching responsibilities.
- However, there is room for improvement in his written reports which show some inattention to detail and are not always put together logically.

Forced ranking

While there is some reluctance to abandon rating there seems to be much more interest in abolishing forced ranking, also known as 'stack-ranking' systems. Forced ranking first achieved fame when it was used by Jack Welch at General Electric to identify poor performers. He argued: 'A company that bets its future on its people must remove the lower 10 per cent, and keep removing it every year – always raising the bar of performance and increasing the quality of its leadership' (General Electric Company, 2000).

Supporters of forced ranking say it is a good way of weeding out unsatisfactory employees as well as identifying and rewarding the top players – but it doesn't really work. Arkin (2007) noted that 'before imploding, thanks to the actions of its own top performers, Enron used a complicated system to rank and yank its employees'. The 'rank and yank' approach may have its advocates, but Meisler (2003), in an article tellingly called 'Dead man's curve', thought that: 'For most people – especially those with outmoded concepts of loyalty and job security – the prospect of Darwinian struggle at the work place is not a happy one.'

Research conducted by Garcia, as reported in *Machine Design* (2007), established that in forced ranking systems individuals will care less about performing well on a given task and instead shift their focus to performing relatively better on a scale. Those ranked highest on the scale are more competitive and less cooperative than those ranked lower.

A further difficulty is that when an organization gets rid of the bottom 10 per cent a proportion of those in the average category will drop down automatically into the unsatisfactory category without any change in their level of performance. As Ed Lawler, quoted by Aguinis (2005) commented, if a prescribed percentage of employees is let go every year because they have been placed in the 'C' category, this will at some time cut into the 'bone' of the organization. Research by Meisler (2003) found that for this reason, after about three iterations, forced distribution systems became ineffective. A simulation by Scullen *et al* (2005) established that while there were improvements in performance in the first few years of the operation of forced ranking this drains away and eventually becomes zero. O'Malley (2003) described forced ranking as a 'gross method of categorizing employees into a few evaluative buckets'.

A mechanistic 'rank and yank' system will only create a climate of fear and will at best inhibit and at worst destroy any possibility that performance management is perceived and used as a developmental process. This is illustrated by the experience of stack-ranking at Microsoft, as reported by Kurt Eichenwald (2012):

> Under the stack-ranking system at Microsoft, managers graded their subordinates according to a bell curve. Top performers got a grade of 1; bottom performers a grade of 5. Bonuses were directed to high scorers. Bottom scorers got reassignment or the boot. The curve dictated that every group – even one made up entirely of all-stars – would have its share of 5s.

Stack-ranking created an inward-looking culture more focused on back-stabbing and office politics than on the outside world. Every current and former Microsoft employee interviewed by Eichenwald cited stack-ranking as the most destructive process inside of Microsoft. A former Microsoft software developer said: 'It leads to employees focusing on competing with each other, rather than competing with other companies.' Each year the intensity and destructiveness of the game-playing grew worse as employees struggled to beat their co-workers for promotions, bonuses, or just survival: 'In the end, the stack-ranking system crippled the ability to innovate at Microsoft.' As noted in Chapter 4, Microsoft has since taken account of this reaction and abandoned rating completely.

Performance pay decisions without ranking

Twenty per cent of the respondents to the e-reward survey of contingent pay (2004) did without ratings. Some companies adopted what might be called a 'holistic method'. Managers proposed where people should be placed in the pay range for their grade, taking into account their contribution and pay relative to others in similar jobs, their potential and the relationship of their current pay to market rates. The decision may be expressed in the form of a statement that an individual is now worth £30,000 rather than £28,000. The increase is 7 per cent, but what counts is the overall view about the value of a person to the organization, not the percentage increase to that person's pay.

A common approach is to 'decouple' performance pay from performance reviews or appraisals (ie conduct pay reviews separately and on a different date). Managers would then be asked simply to recommend the size of the increase, eg high, average, low or none, based on their assessment of the value of the individual to the organization. A measure of forced distribution may be introduced, for example, no more than 20 per cent to receive a high increase, 60 per cent to receive an average increase and 20 per cent to receive a smaller or no increase. The percentage increases to be awarded in each category would be determined centrally in accordance with the pay review budget. This is, of course, a form of assessment, but it is not presented in crude A, B, C, etc, terms as part of a performance review.

At Gap Inc, with the removal of ratings, employees are no longer awarded a grade at the end of the year. Managers do not have to force people into categories but are still required to differentiate employee performance when allocating their merit and bonus pot. The reward discussion is separated from any discussion of performance. Instead of having one lengthy conversation at the end of the year that tried to cover performance and reward, there are now 12 performance conversations throughout the year and one brief rewards conversation at the end of the year. All the manager needs to say is: 'Here's how the company did, here's how our business unit did, here's a reminder of a couple of things you did really well and a couple of places where you are still developing – now here's your money.' If managers have done their job, regularly discussing performance during the year, there should be no surprises. It's much easier than the long and sometimes contentious conversations managers used to have.

Identifying potential

Procedures are necessary for identifying people who are qualified for membership of a talent pool or who have the potential to become members after completing a talent management development programme. It is usual for assessments of potential to be made initially by the individual's line manager. Traditionally assessments have been made as part of an annual performance review and have been associated with ranking. If ranking is abandoned it is still necessary to identify and classify people according to assessments of their potential as the starting point of a talent management programme – performance management plays a major role in talent management, not only in identifying talent but also in establishing development needs.

The identification and classification of potential can be carried out by the line manager using a simple three-box method, for example: 'emerging', 'growing' or 'high' potential; or 'ready now to progress beyond current grade', 'could progress beyond current grade within two years' or 'best suited to current grade'. If a 'check-in' procedure is used, involving informal discussions on performance throughout the year rather than a formal annual review, a separate potential assessment may be necessary.

There are two problems with this approach to assessing potential. First, line managers may be reasonably good at assessing performance in the present job but they are not as well qualified to judge potential to carry out higher level jobs because they may not be aware of the requirements for their successful performance. Second, high performance in the current job may contribute to high potential but does not necessarily equate with it.

To deal with these problems it is necessary to do three things. First, clarify the criteria to be used for assessing potential – these should be those adopted for defining the qualifications for membership of a talent pool; second, train line managers who make potential assessments in how to apply the criteria; and third, consider using the nine-box grid. This is a widely adopted approach to identifying talent: over half of the organizations studied by Campbell and Hirsh (2013) were using it or were planning to introduce it in the future. As illustrated in Figure 8.4, the grid uses two axes – performance and potential – with three levels on each axis, forming nine boxes in total.

Whatever approach to assessing potential is adopted it is important to ensure that the line manager discusses it with the individual, explaining the reason for the assessment and giving performance feedback. This should be two-way conversation in which the individual has the opportunity to comment. It should lead to a general

Figure 8.4   A nine-point performance/potential assessment grid

		Performance		
		Low	Medium	High
Potential	**High**	Shows every sign of the potential to go further but is under-performing in the present role.	Has the potential to go further. Performance is at an acceptable level.	Demonstrates high potential. Regularly achieves challenging and stretching goals.
	Medium	Capable of taking on greater responsibilities if there is a significant improvement in performance.	Has the potential to keep developing and to deliver more in either scale or complexity. Performance is acceptable.	Capable of growing into a higher level role in due course. A consistently strong performer, delivering excellent value.
	Low	No potential for growth beyond this level. Is seriously under-performing in the present role.	Valued in current role but is not expected to advance beyond this level. Generally meets performance expectations.	Highly valued at this level and in current role. A strong performer who is a core team member.

discussion on the career prospects of the individual. If there is room for performance improvement the aim should be to reach an agreement on what needs to be done – by the individual *and* by the manager.

Conclusions

1   The disadvantages of rating considerably outweigh the advantages. As an HR Director told Armstrong and Baron (1998): 'Rating denigrates the whole performance management process.' Rating should therefore be abandoned.

2   Forced ranking systems are pernicious and should not be used.

3   Performance and development reviews would focus on the future, setting goals and agreeing development needs and the actions required to satisfy them. They would not incorporate ratings.

4 Organizations that cannot bear the idea of some form of performance assessment could consider using visual assessment or performance commentaries.

5 There are perfectly effective methods of deciding on performance pay increases without the use of crude overall ratings.

6 Similarly, there are good ways of identifying potential in the absence of overall ratings.

References

Aguinis, H (2005) *Performance Management*, Pearson Education, Upper Saddle River, NJ

Arkin, A (2007) Force for good? *People Management*, 8 February, pp 26–29

Armstrong, M and Baron, A (1998) *Performance Management: The new realities*, CIPD, London

Campbell, V and Hirsh W (2013) *Talent Management: A four-step approach* http://www.employment-studies.co.uk/system/files/resources/files/502.pdf (accessed 14 January 2016)

Coens, T and Jenkins, M (2002) *Abolishing Performance Appraisals: Why they backfire and what to do instead*, Berrett-Koehler, San Francisco, CA

DeNisi, A S and Pritchard, R D (2006) Performance appraisal, performance management and improving individual performance: a motivational framework, *Management and Organization Review*, **2** (2), pp 253–77

Eichenwald, K (2012) *Microsoft's Lost Decade*, http://www.vanityfair.com/business/2012/08/microsoft (accessed 8 April 2016)

e-reward (2004) *Contingent Pay Survey*, e-reward, Stockport

e-reward (2014) *Survey of Performance Management*, e-reward, Stockport

Fletcher, C (2001) Performance appraisal and management: the developing research agenda, *Journal of Occupational and Organizational Psychology*, **74** (4), pp 473–87

Furnham, A (2004) Performance management systems, *European Business Journal*, **16** (2), pp 83–94

General Electric Company (2000) *GE 2000 Annual Report*, http://www.ge.coni/annualOO/letter/index.html (accessed 8 April 2016)

Grote, D (1996) *The Complete Guide to Performance Appraisal*, Amacom, New York

Hofherr, J (2015) What really happens when companies kill performance reviews, Boston.com, www.boston.com/jobs/jobs-news/2015/11/17/what-really-happens-when-companies-kill-performance-reviews (accessed 9 April 2016)

Jawahar, I M and Williams, C R (1997) Where all children are above average: the performance appraisal purpose effect, *Personnel Psychology*, 50, pp 905–25

Lee, C D (2005) Rethinking the goals of your performance management system, *Employment Relations Today*, 32 (3), pp 53–60

Machine Design (2007) Forced ranking of employees bad for business (editorial), September, pp 2–3

Meisler, A (2003) Dead man's curve, *Workforce Management*, June, pp 44–49

Murphy, K R and Cleveland, J (1995) *Understanding Performance Appraisal*, Sage, London

O'Malley, M (2003) Forced ranking, *WorldatWork Journal*, First Quarter, pp 31–39

Pulakos, E D, Mueller-Hanson, R A and O'Leary, R S (2008) Performance management in the US, in (eds) A Varma, P S Budhwar and A DeNisi, *Performance Management Systems: A global perspective*, Routledge, Abingdon

Roberts, E R (1994) Maximizing performance appraisal system acceptance: perspectives from municipal government personnel administrators, *Public Personnel Management*, 23 (4), pp 525–48

Saffie-Robertson, M C and Brutus, S (2014) The impact of interdependence on performance evaluations: the mediating role of discomfort with performance appraisal, *The International Journal of Human Resource Management*, 25 (3), pp 459–73

Scullen, S E and Mount, M K (2000) Understanding the latent structure of job performance ratings, *Journal of Applied Psychology*, 85 (6) pp 956–70

Scullen, S E, Bergey, P K and Aiman-Smith, L (2005) Forced distribution ratings and the improvement of workforce potential: a baseline simulation, *Personnel Psychology*, 58 (1), pp 1–31

Silverman, M, Kerrin, M and Carter, A (2005) *360-degree Feedback: Beyond the spin*, Institute for Employment Studies, Brighton

Strebler, M T, Bevan, S and Robertson D (2001) *Performance Review: Balancing objectives and content*, Institute for Employment Studies, Brighton

Wherry, R J and Bartlett, C J (1982) The control of bias in ratings: a theory of rating, *Personnel Psychology*, 35 (3), pp 521–51

Enhance personal development

Introduction

Reinventing performance management is not just about abolishing the annual review and ratings, although it is important to do so. It is also about ensuring that performance management achieves its purpose of developing people so that they can make a greater contribution to the success and prosperity of their organization and also advance their careers. As Lawler *et al* (2012) noted: 'A key issue for any performance management system is how effectively it identifies the skill needs of individuals and assures that they are adequate.'

This chapter first examines the concept of continuous development, which can be associated with performance and development conversations or check-ins as described in Chapter 7. It then focuses on the key development process of coaching and the skills required by managers in their capacity as coaches.

Continuous development

Developing people is a continuous process. Traditionally, personal development plans were produced by managers for their staff, because that is what HR wanted. Having gone through the motions they were forgotten, except possibly for the occasional formal training course. It is far better to use informal performance and development conversations (PDCs) or check-ins that can take place fairly frequently rather than agreeing a formal development plan once a year.

The development aspect of the conversation identifies any emerging learning needs and discusses how they can be satisfied. The focus should be on promoting self-managed learning, which takes place when individuals take responsibility for meeting their own learning needs with help and guidance from their managers or learning and development specialists as necessary. This is the most effective method of learning. However, the development conversation may highlight a need for coaching to develop skills that are specific to the work the individual carries out now or may be required to do in the future. This coaching is best provided by the manager or team leader, who needs to be encouraged to carry out this important part of his or her duties. He or she also needs help in developing coaching skills. Ideally this should be provided by learning and development specialists in the form of coaching (being coached is one good way of learning how to coach if the lessons learnt from the experience are brought out and explained). More formal training events can be used as long as they involve plenty of practical sessions, including role plays.

Development conversations should *not* just be about identifying training needs and the suitable formal courses to satisfy them. Training courses may form part of a learning programme plan, but a minor part; coaching and other learning activities such as those listed below are much more important:

- adopting a role model (mentor);
- observing and analysing what others do (good practice);
- extending the role (job enrichment);
- project work, special assignments;
- involvement in other work areas;
- involvement in communities of practice (learning from others carrying out similar work);
- action learning;
- e-learning;
- guided reading.

Coaching

Coaching is possibly the most effective way of providing continuous development and line managers are well positioned to do this. Coaching is a personal (usually one-to-one) method of helping people to develop their skills and levels of competence. The need for coaching may arise from formal or informal performance reviews but opportunities for coaching will emerge during normal day-to-day activities. Every time a manager delegates a new task to someone a coaching opportunity is created to help the individual learn any new skills or techniques needed to get the job done. Every time a manager provides feedback to an individual after a task has been completed there is an opportunity to help that individual do better next time. Coaching as part of the normal process of management consists of:

- Making people aware of how well they are performing by, for example, asking them questions to establish the extent to which they have thought through what they are doing.

- Controlled delegation – ensuring that individuals not only know what is expected of them but also understand what they need to know and be able to do to complete the task satisfactorily. This gives managers an opportunity to provide guidance at the outset; guidance at a later stage may be seen as interference.

- Using whatever situations that may arise as opportunities to promote learning.

- Encouraging people to look at higher-level problems and how they would tackle them.

As Lee (2005) explained: 'The coaching model of performance management redefines the relationship between the supervisor and the subordinate. The two work together to help the subordinate perform at his or her very best.' Coaching involves short-term interventions designed to remedy problems that interfere with the employee's performance but it is also concerned with longer-term development and continuous learning.

The process of coaching

As described by the CIPD (2007), coaching is essentially a non-directive form of development. Evered and Selman (1989) defined the following essential characteristics that define good coaching: developing a partnership, commitment to producing a result, responsiveness to people, practice and preparation, a sensitivity to individuals, and a willingness to go beyond what has already been achieved. Woodruffe (2008) suggested that coaching should aim to:

- amplify an individual's own knowledge and thought processes;
- improve the individual's self-awareness and facilitate the winning of detailed insight into how the individual may be perceived by others;
- create a supportive, helpful, yet demanding, environment in which the individual's crucial thinking skills, ideas and behaviours are challenged and developed.

Techniques of coaching

Good coaching is about encouraging people to think through issues, getting them to see things differently, enabling them to work out solutions for themselves that they can 'own', and empowering them to do things differently. Hallbom and Warrenton-Smith (2005) recommend the following coaching techniques:

- Ask high-impact questions – 'how' and 'what' open-ended questions that spur action rather than 'why' questions that require explanations.
- Help people to develop their own answers and action plans.
- Identify what people are doing right and then make the most of it rather than just trying to fix problems – coaching is success-driven.
- Build rapport and trust – make it safe for employees to express their concerns and ideas.
- Get employees to work out answers for themselves – people often resist being *told* what to do or how to do it.

Coaching skills

A good coach is one who questions and listens. Coaching will be most effective when the coach understands that his or her role is to help people to learn and individuals are motivated to learn. They should be aware that their present level of knowledge or skill or their behaviour needs to be improved if they are going to perform their work to their own and to other's satisfaction. Individuals should be given guidance on what they should be learning, feedback on how they are doing and, because learning is an active not a passive process, they should be actively involved with their coach who should be constructive, building on strengths and experience.

Feedback and coaching

A check-in or feedback session can be used as an opportunity for coaching when it involves:

- Noting what has gone well so that a basis is provided for further development.
- Identifying areas where performance outcomes show that there are aspects of knowledge and skills that should be developed.
- Providing instant advice or guidance on what needs to be done.
- Indicating any learning need that can be met by further coaching or other form of development.

Coaching through delegation

Delegation is an effective method of coaching. It is a natural part of what managers do and it provides a great opportunity for people to develop new skills or extend existing ones. The process of controlled delegation can indicate to managers where people need guidance and help. To make the most of delegation, managers should ensure that individuals understand:

- why the work needs to be done;
- what they are expected to do;

- how they are expected to do it;
- the date by which they are expected to do it;
- the authority they have to make decisions;
- the problems they must refer back;
- the progress or completion reports they should submit;
- how you propose to guide and monitor them;
- the resources and help they will have available to complete the work.

People may need guidance on how the work should be done. The extent to which this is necessary will clearly depend on how much they already know about how to do the work. Managers should not give directions in such laborious detail that they run the risk of stifling initiative. As long as they are sure that individuals can do the job they should let them get on with it.

Conclusions

The conclusions reached in this chapter are: reinventing performance management is not just about abolishing the annual review and ratings, although it is important to do so. It is also about ensuring that performance management achieves its true purpose: developing people so that they can make a greater contribution to the success and prosperity of their organization and advance their careers.

Continuous development

- It is far better to use informal PDCs or check-ins that can take place fairly frequently than to agree a formal development plan once a year.
- The development aspect of the conversation identifies any emerging learning needs and discusses how they can be satisfied. The focus should be on promoting self-managed learning, which takes place when individuals take responsibility for meeting their own learning needs with help and guidance from their managers or

learning and development specialists as necessary. This is the most effective method of learning.

Coaching

- Continuous development can be enhanced by coaching, and line managers are well positioned to do this.

- Coaching is a personal (usually one-to-one) method of helping people to develop their skills and levels of competence.

- The need for coaching may arise from formal or informal performance reviews but opportunities for coaching will emerge during normal day-to-day activities.

References

Chartered Institute of Personnel and Development (2007) *Coaching Fact Sheet*, CIPD, London

Evered, R D and Selman, J C (1989) Coaching and the art of management, *Organizational Dynamics*, **18** (2), pp 16–32

Hallbom, T and Warrenton-Smith, A (2005) The manager as coach, *Journal of Innovative Management*, Summer, pp 39–48

Lawler, E E, Benson, G S and McDermott, M (2012) What makes performance appraisals effective? *Compensation & Benefits Review*, **44** (4), pp 191–200

Lee, C D (2005) Rethinking the goals of your performance management system, *Employment Relations Today*, **32** (3), pp 53–60

Woodruffe, C (2008) Could do better? *Must* do better! *British Journal of Administrative Management*, January, pp 14–16

Provide training 10

Introduction

Throughout this book the need for training both line managers and employees generally in performance management processes and skills has been emphasized. Performance management does not work when managers don't believe it's worth doing or, even when they do, they lack the skills to do it properly. Employees also need to know why performance management is important, and they require training in objective setting and using feedback. In this chapter consideration is given to how such training can be provided. Examples of training workshops are also given.

Formal learning

Formal performance management training can take place in half- or full-day workshops. Other methods as practised by respondents to the e-reward survey (2014) are:

- coaching from HR and the leadership team;
- online training (e-learning);
- practical case-study examples;
- roadshows.

The typical subjects covered by the training were:

- evaluation and assessment skills;
- how to give feedback;
- how to deal with 'difficult' conversations;
- attaining consistency and avoiding bias;

- achieving quality rather than just quantity;
- regular updates of business objectives.

Methods

PowerPoint slides with attached notes may be used to present some of the material formally. However, learning, especially skills development, is best achieved by participative methods – guided discussions, role plays and other exercises – although it can take place through by e-learning.

Guided discussion

The aim of guided discussions would be to get participants to think through for themselves the learning points. For example, when covering review meetings the trainer asks questions such as:

- What do you think makes for a good review meeting? Can you provide any examples from your previous experience?
- What do you think can go wrong with a meeting? Have you any instances?
- Why is it important to create the right environment?
- How do you set about doing so?
- What sort of things should be discussed in a review meeting?
- Why is it important for managers to let the individual do most of the talking?
- Why could self-assessment be useful?

Role plays

Role plays are usually based on a written brief that defines the same situation from each participant's point of view so that they can understand what it feels like to be in either position.

Workshop members are then asked to play out the roles and fellow members assess their performance (this in itself provides some practice in performance assessment). Each person playing the role will also describe his or her feelings about the review, and assess the other person's performance or behaviour.

Role plays are particularly useful as a means of developing skills in conducting performance and development conversations (check-ins), providing feedback and handling challenging meetings.

Exercises

Exercises can be used to enable participants to practise their skills. For example, practice in goal setting could take place by dividing the course members into pairs and getting then to agree in turn on each óther's role profile, goals and key performance indicators.

Workshops

Formal training can be provided in workshops, which concentrate on developing skills. The following subjects could be covered in half-day workshops or combined for longer programmes:

1 conducting performance and development conversations;
2 providing feedback;
3 setting objectives;
4 handling challenging conversations;
5 coaching.

Examples of the approaches that can be used in each of these areas are given below.

WORKSHOP 1: CHECK-INS

Introductory presentation

- A performance and development conversation (PDC) is an informal conversation between a manager and an individual that takes place at periodical intervals (at least quarterly) or as required, to discuss the latter's progress and future development.

- It is an important means of managing performance by ensuring that individuals are aware of their strengths and how to use and develop them, and understand any aspects of their work where improvements are required and what can be done about them.

- Check-ins involve the provision of feedback as a basis for discussing development needs.

- Check-ins should be positive events but they may have to deal with performance problems and this could mean having to handle a challenging conversation.

- Use check-ins as opportunities to define or redefine objectives and to initiate or amend development plans.

- Check-ins do not involve any rating of performance.

- The outcome of a check-in is not recorded on a report or form, but notes on any proposed actions can be useful.

Presentation: How to conduct a PDC

Overall approach

- The PDC should be conducted informally. It should be seen by both the manager and the individual as simply part (although an important part) of the normal process of working together. It should not be treated as a special event.

- The PDC should include positive feedback with an emphasis on strengths rather than weaknesses.

- It should be forward looking – about future actions to enhance performance and meet development needs rather than a post-mortem on the past.

- However, if there are performance problems these should be identified and discussed and actions agreed to remedy them. Actions to improve performance can be taken by the individual with whatever help and guidance required from the managers. Where skills need to be developed the actions required in the shape of coaching or training can be identified. Note that serious under-performance problems should be dealt with as they arise – they should not wait for a check-in.

Always end the PDC on a positive note.

Examples of questions

The following are examples of positive questions that can be put by the manager:

- How well do you feel you have done?
- What do you feel are your strengths?
- What do you like most about your job?
- Why do you think that project went well?
- What ideas do you have about your future?
- Is there anything you feel you need to learn to do even better in your present job or to develop your career?

The following are examples of the questions that might be put by a manager if there have been performance problems:

- Why do you think you didn't meet that target?
- What do you think went wrong?
- What can be done to prevent it happening again?

Role play: Conducting a PDC

Brief for the practice leader, HR group

Freeman, Reynolds and Waring (FRW) is a major international firm of accountants and management consultants. Its largest consultancy divisions are responsible for financial management, IT and retail services. There is also a small but developing HR management consultancy group. FRW has an excellent reputation as a place to launch or develop a career. It has no difficulty in attracting well-qualified and talented people.

FRW has a reputation for exacting high standards of performance. Its current performance management system was introduced recently to replace an outdated performance appraisal procedure. The main innovation was to replace the annual formal performance review with relatively informal 'check-ins' that take place between practice leaders and individual consultants who are permanent members of their teams.

You are Pat Thomas, practice leader for the HR group with a team of eight consultants. They may work for you on HR projects that may be only concerned with HR matters but may be inter-disciplinary teams covering a wider range of areas in an organizational review project. Practice leaders are responsible for the continuing management and development of their own team of consultants. Your consultants may be assigned to consultancy projects controlled by another project leader on an inter-disciplinary team, and for the duration of the project are responsible to that project leader.

Alex Wright joined your team 12 months ago as an HR consultant. Alex had eight years' good HR experience and is well qualified with a 2.1 degree in history from Manchester University and an MA in human resource management from DeMontfort University, plus chartered membership of the CIPD.

Alex attended the one-week standard consultancy skills learning programme but because of your other commitments has not been given the amount of guidance and help you would have liked to provide and has therefore been thrown in the deep end on three assignments for which you have been responsible. Fortunately, the first two assignments were not too testing. Alex's role was mainly supportive and did not involve any major responsibilities for producing recommendations or writing reports, and Alex did reasonably well. However, the most recent assignment was a large one that involved an inter-disciplinary team of consultants and you had to spend most of your time sorting out how to coordinate their activities and therefore had little time to provide any guidance to Alex, who had to deal with and report on the HR aspects of the projects and liaise with the other consultants and the client.

In spite of this lack of guidance Alex did not do too badly, showing initiative, good analytical skills and the ability to arrive at innovative and practical conclusions. However, there have been problems. You had to point out on two occasions, which you noted, that more cooperation was needed with the client and the other team members – accountants and IT specialists, and the HR aspects of the project should not be tackled as a separate entity. You were also somewhat dissatisfied with the quality of Alex's report writing, which needed quite a lot of re-drafting.

The major inter-disciplinary assignment has just been successfully completed – it lasted three months. You are now about to conduct a post-project PDC with Alex. You want to discuss how the project went and how Alex sees the future. You think that Alex is potentially a very good consultant and that the initial problems will easily be overcome with more guidance from you than has been provided so far. You may be able to discuss any further training that would help.

Brief for the management consultant

You are Alex Wright a management consultant in the HR practice of French, Reynolds and Waring (FRW) a major international firm of accountants and management consultants. You have had eight years' good experience as an HR assistant and then an HR business partner in a large financial institution in the City. You have a 2:1 degree in history from Manchester University and an MA in human resource management from DeMontfort University, plus chartered membership of the CIPD. You joined FRW as an HR consultant 12 months ago in its small but growing HR practice. You saw this as a great opportunity to develop your career.

Your experience so far in has been mixed. You had a brief (one week) learning programme in consultancy skills six weeks after you had joined, which was quite helpful but you felt it was rather superficial on such aspects as client relationships and report writing. You were given very little responsibility on your first two assignments controlled by your practice leader, Pat Thomas. You were then flung into the deep end on a major multi-disciplinary assignment, also controlled by Pat Thomas who, however, was so involved in liaising with a rather demanding and difficult client and controlling the other consultants, who had not worked together before, that you were left mainly to your own devices to deal with some quite critical HR issues with little guidance or help. You have found it difficult to work with other team members who do not seem to understand the important contribution the HR aspect can make to the success of the project and are too preoccupied with their own parts of the project to pay you much attention. Neither have relationships with the client been too easy. They want to talk to Pat Thomas, not you. Pat Thomas may have spent little time with you but did point out on two occasions that better cooperation was needed with other team members and that he had some adverse comments from the client about your contribution. Although how they were in a position to make such comments when their contacts with you had been so superficial, you don't understand. One of the client's senior managers was indeed dismissive when you made a suggestion but you don't think he really understood what you were getting at.

You have also had problems in drafting reports in accordance with the rather rigid guidelines of FRW and you had to do quite a lot of re-drafting. You have never had problems in report writing before but you recognize that you previously may not have had to conform to the very high standards expected by the firm.

Clearly there have been a number of problems with this assignment but you feel that these arose because you had received inadequate training and guidance. In terms of report writing, you feel that you are learning fast to accommodate yourself to the FRW requirements. You simply don't understand or accept the criticism that your team orientation and interpersonal skills are inadequate.

Overall, you have very mixed feelings about your time with FRW. You have enjoyed the challenge of consultancy and you find the present assignment stimulating, but you are highly critical of the way you were treated initially and this has soured the relationship. You would like to continue but you may need some persuading. You know that your old firm would take you back tomorrow in a more senior position. You are about to attend a 'PDC' with Pat Thomas. This will be your first PDC, which you understand is FRW-speak for what in your past organization you would have called a 'performance review'.

WORKSHOP 2: PROVIDING FEEDBACK

Presentation

What is feedback?

Feedback is the provision of information to people on how they have performed in terms of results, events, critical incidents and significant behaviours.

Why is feedback important?

Feedback lets people know how they are doing and what they can do to improve their performance. It plays a key role, along with goal setting, in the self-regulation of performance. Feedback focuses attention on performance goals that are important to the organization, helps discover errors, maintains direction in achieving goals, influences new goals, provides information on performance capabilities and on how much more effort/energy is needed to reach goals, and provides positive reinforcement for goal accomplishments.

What is meant by positive and negative feedback?

- Feedback is positive and helpful when it recognizes success, or constructive when it identifies areas for improvement that can lead to effective action.
- It is negative and unhelpful when perceived failings are dwelt on as matters for blame.
- A positive approach is to treat mistakes or errors of judgement as opportunities for learning so that they are less likely to be repeated in the future.

What are the requirements for successful feedback?

- Build feedback into the job – clarify key performance indicators.
- Provide feedback on actual events at the time.
- Describe, don't judge.
- Be non-threatening.

- Address performance issues; do not make it personal.
- Refer to and define specific behaviours.
- Define good work or behaviour.
- Provide positive and constructive feedback.
- Ask questions.
- Select key issues.
- Focus on how the task was tackled, not just the results.
- Ensure feedback leads to action.

When should feedback be given?

Feedback will be most effective and have the greatest impact if it is delivered as soon after the event as possible while the situation is fresh in everyone's mind. If action is not taken quickly the employee could be misled by being given the impression that there is no problem and would be denied the chance to improve or put things right.

What should managers avoid doing when they provide feedback?

- Focus only on what has been achieved, not dealing with how it was achieved.
- Offer opinions rather than facts.
- Make personal attacks.

What is the best way for a manager to convey to an employee that his or her performance has not been up to standard?

Always base the message on recent factual evidence.

Role play: A feedback session at Middlemarch Garden Centre

Brief for the general manager

You are Sam Williams, the owner and general manager of Middlemarch Garden Centre. Your task is to conduct a feedback 'check-in' meeting with Vivian Farnham who manages the new products section of the garden centre.

Middlemarch Garden Centre has been trading for the last 15 years. Set within easy reach of Manchester and the better-off parts of Cheshire and with a flourishing online sales operation it has grown from a smallish nursery started by the present owner's father to a substantial business with a turnover of £80 million a year. The company now employs over 400 people.

The most recent development is the introduction of fresh produce sales, an activity that has been running for nine months under the management of Vivian Farnham, who was recruited especially for this post.

An HR manager was recruited two years ago and, amongst other innovations, introduced a basic performance review scheme involving an annual review meeting that is mainly concerned with providing feedback on performance and discussing any performance improvement plans that may be necessary. Performance is not rated.

You inherited the Middlemarch Garden Centre two years ago from your father and continue to act as general manager. You are anxious to expand the business and, besides developing online sales of plants and other garden products and installing an improved website, nine months ago you set up a new department in which a wide variety of fresh food products would be procured and then sold in a specially designed separate store at the garden centre. You have been spending a great deal of money on promoting the new produce venture in local papers and radio, through leaflets and the website.

You recruited Vivian Farnham a year ago to set up and run the new section. Vivian seemed to be the best candidate with four years' experience working on the fresh produce side in a supermarket chain in a fairly junior role concerned with sourcing and purchasing a range of meat products but with no experience in managing staff and little experience in selling apart from an initial three months in-store experience. Despite the latter drawbacks, Vivian appeared to have the personal qualities and drive to be a success running the new produce section.

You are pleased with the way Vivian buys. The price and quality seem to be right, and Vivian has good ideas about merchandising

– how to make the section attractive. However, there are problems. It is apparent that the section will only just break even. If capital and below-the-line publicity costs are taken into account the whole venture looks in danger of not being viable. It is, admittedly, early days and there are three months to go to the year-end in June.

One problem is footfall – the number of people entering the shopping area in a given time. This started well and was good just before Christmas, but it is declining. As footfall diminishes so do sales. Sales per square foot of selling space have gone down by 12 per cent since Christmas – considerably below budget.

The new produce store is run on a day-to-day basis by an experienced sales person with one full-time assistant and one part-timer. Temporary staff are engaged for weekends and peak selling periods. Vivian is concerned with merchandising – presenting the goods in the store – and is good at it, but has little direct contact with customers. You think that this lack of contact may contribute to the relatively poor sales performance.

Another problem is the amount of product waste that is being generated: at 15 per cent of total purchasing cost it is well above the accepted maximum of 10 per cent. Is Vivian buying too much stock that cannot be sold before it deteriorates? Do Vivian's product ordering and control practices need to improve?

You think that the way Vivian handles the department's staff may be at the root of the problem. They have all been appointed by Vivian. You believe that the staff are not really engaged with their work or well-motivated. Vivian is rather remote, concentrating on sourcing, merchandising and promotion activities. Although Vivian spends quite a lot of time in the shop, you have observed that much of it is devoted to criticizing the staff rather than motivating them. You believe that the staff feel they are treated as second-class citizens. Indeed your brother-in-law, whose daughter Jenny works in the store at weekends, spoke to you a couple of weeks ago, asking: 'What's up with Vivian who seems to have a power complex and is always ordering people around?' and remarking that Jenny 'likes the money but doesn't like working in the store'.

You are now planning how to conduct a formal feedback session with Vivian as part of the performance review scheme that has recently been introduced. You will want to recognize strong points, namely the way Vivian buys – the price and quality seem to be right – and Vivian has good ideas about merchandising – how to make the section and its products attractive to customer.

You have already gone through the business results in detail but you intend to remind Vivian that they need to improve and that you want to discuss any issues that may explain the situation. Your aim is to get Vivian to accept that there are problems in the ways in which the section is being managed as a basis for a future discussion on what can be done about them. The problems you will want to raise are: the high level of waste, and staff management difficulties.

Brief for the manager, new produce department

You are Vivian Farnham. You manage the new produce department of Middlemarch Garden Centre. Your task is to take part in a performance feedback 'check-in' meeting with your boss, Sam Williams, who is the owner and general manager of the centre.

Middlemarch Garden Centre has been trading for the last 15 years. Set within easy reach of Manchester and the better-off parts of Cheshire and with a flourishing online sales operation it has grown from a smallish nursery started by the present owner's father to a substantial business with a turnover of £80 million a year. The company now employs over 400 people.

The most recent development is the introduction of fresh produce sales, an activity that has been running for nine months under your management; you were recruited especially for this post.

An HR manager was recruited two years ago and, amongst other innovations, introduced a basic performance review scheme involving an annual review meeting that is mainly concerned with providing feedback on performance and discussing any performance improvement plans that may be necessary. Performance is not rated.

You were recruited a year ago by the owner and general manager of Middlemarch Garden Centre, Sam Williams, to start up and manage the fresh produce department in which a wide variety of food products would be procured and then sold through a specially designed separate store at the garden centre. Sam Williams told you that a great deal of money was being spent on promoting the new produce venture in local papers and radio, through leaflets and the website.

After graduating with a 2:2 business studies degree four years ago you worked as an intern in the head office of a large supermarket chain and were fortunate enough to be offered a job as a trainee meat products buyer. Your role was to assist in the sourcing and purchasing of a range of meat products, but you gained no experience in managing staff and little experience in selling apart from an initial three months in-store experience. Your last appraisal there was good – you were congratulated on your drive and initiative. You joined Middlemarch Garden Centre because it seemed to offer you a great opportunity to develop and manage a profit centre, albeit small at first, but with plenty of growth potential within the centre and indeed elsewhere.

When you started it was made clear that the produce venture had to make a profit in the first year. Nine months after the section opened it is apparent that you will be lucky to break even if things continue as they are. Your trading income will cover costs but no more. You are unhappy about the way the new produce shop has been publicized and you are certain that the problem stems from poor footfall: not enough customers walking through the door. Sales per square foot of selling space have gone down by 12 per cent since Christmas – considerably below budget. But Middlemarch is well placed to attract high spending customers from the affluent areas of South Manchester and Cheshire.

You have bought well, locally from wholesalers and to a small extent direct from the markets. Quality has been good and you believe you have provided a good product range to attract trade. In particular, in the run-up to Christmas your selection of exotic fruit and vegetables was well received.

As you approach your performance review with your boss, Sam Williams, you want to press for more publicity to increase footfall. You also want to spend more on high quality, unusual products to supplement the standard range. If the public were more aware of your existence and came to try you out they would find a good range of quality products and then, you believe, sales turnover would soar. You also want to take time to develop more local growers as suppliers for the standard fruit and vegetables. These would, you hope, give better service and better quality for the price than the major wholesalers.

You know that there has been a problem with product wastage – it reached 15 per cent of total purchasing cost during the last quarter, well above the accepted maximum of 10 per cent. You are reasonably satisfied that you are making the right choice of product mix, quantity, quality and price but you are making every effort to improve the ratio by carefully reviewing your buying and stocking policies.

You believe that an important reason for the problem is that the shop staff are not sufficiently engaged with their work and seem incapable of taking any initiative. All are young and their standards of housekeeping and display are poor. They get on well with customers but their selling skills are inadequate. You have told them they must improve, to no effect. You are afraid to spend time away from the shop for fear of what they might do in your absence. You have to tell them absolutely everything that has to be done; you would think they would pick up some of it. You are wondering whether to take disciplinary action against them unless their attitudes and performance change for the better. Their timekeeping leaves much to be desired and there have been too many sick days.

At your meeting you will want to raise the possibility of more sales promotions and your ideas about product development. You will explain that you believe that you have wastage under control. You will also want to raise the problem of the performance of your staff and the possibility of disciplinary action to persuade them to improve.

WORKSHOP 3: OBJECTIVE SETTING

Introductory presentation

- Setting objectives is a key performance management activity.
- Objectives define the direction people should take and provide the criteria needed to assess performance and the basis for identifying development needs.

- The process of setting objectives for a role should be carried out jointly by the manager and the role-holder. It involves the following steps:

  - Define the purpose of the job or role and the main activities carried out to achieve that purpose (usually not more than five or six). This is usually called a 'role profile'.

  - Decide on the objectives to be achieved for each activity. The objectives can be defined in terms of targets (quantified or specific objectives to be achieved by a certain date) or standards (qualitative definitions of the conditions that will exist when the task has been well done; examples are given below).

  - Consider how to establish that the objectives have been achieved.

Defining a role profile

A role profile consists of a statement of the overall purpose of the role: what it exists to achieve, and a list of the key result areas: the elements of a role (no more than five or six) for which clear outputs and standards exist, each of which makes a significant contribution to achieving its overall purpose.

The key result area definitions should be expressed in a single sentence beginning with an active verb. They should focus on what has to be achieved in that particular area so that they can provide a basis for defining targets or standards. The following is a typical example (preferably this should be one from within the organization concerned).

Role title: Database administrator
Department: Information systems
Overall purpose of role: Responsible for the development and support of databases and their underlying environment

Key result areas

- Identify database requirements for all projects that require data management in order to meet the needs of internal customers.

- Develop project plans collaboratively with colleagues to deliver against their database needs.

- Implement project plans in accordance with defined criteria, within the predefined budget and within the agreed timescale.

- Support underlying database infrastructure to ensure that the level of service delivery required is achieved.

- Ensure security of the database infrastructure through adherence to established protocols and develop additional security protocols where needed.

Defining objectives

Objectives should be:

- Clear.
- Challenging.
- Achievable, but not too easily.
- Measurable, either in quantified or in qualitative terms.
- Agreed.

To define an objective take each key result area in turn and first answer the question: 'What is the role holder expected to achieve in this area of activity?' Where appropriate, this should be a quantified target. If it is not possible to quantify the objective it should be expressed as a performance standard answering the question: 'What are the circumstances when it is evident that the task has been well done?'

Examples of *targets* are:

- Increase successful outcome of cold calls by z per cent by end-February next year.

- Launch product B by end-October this year.

- Complaints from customers should not exceed 1:1,000 transactions.

- Job evaluation appeals should be held within five working days.

Examples of *performance standards* are:

- Performance will be up to standard when data are consistently inputted to the database promptly and accurately.
- Performance will be up to standard when callers are dealt with courteously at all times, even when they are being difficult.
- Performance will be up to standard when line managers obtain guidance on inventory control practice, which makes a significant contribution to the achievement of inventory targets.

To answer the question: 'How will we know that the target or standard has been achieved?' sources such as these can be used:

- returns showing outcomes in the shape of sales volume, production throughput or cost per unit of output;
- data collected on speed of response to enquiries;
- quality control reports showing results against standards and targets;
- statistics on machine downtime;
- information showing that a project has been delivered in accordance with specification, on time and within cost parameters;
- feedback from surveys of internal or external customers;
- levels of engagement as revealed by employee surveys;
- information showing that production schedules and plans are realistic and implemented effectively.

Objective setting, Exercise 1

This exercise provides an introduction to the art of drawing up a role profile from a role analysis and from it defining objectives and key performance indicators. It should be conducted as follows.

---

1 State the aims of the exercise: *To enable participants to understand the purpose and nature of a basic role profile and know how to prepare one. To practise setting objectives.*

2 Issue the transcript of a role analysis interview (see document 1, page 168).

3 Divide the whole group into pairs and ask each pair to work together and, on the basis of the information provided by the role analysis interview, produce a basic role profile with a definition of overall purpose, no more than five or six key result areas and the associated objectives. (45 minutes)

4 Explain that they will have to rearrange the material in the briefing note (the interview transcription) to produce a succinct role profile. Much of the information is about how the work is carried out rather than the results the role holder has to achieve. (This is a typical feature of such an interview, role holders often find it difficult to distinguish between what they do and why they do it.) The superfluous task-based data will have to be eliminated if the result is to be a useable role profile, ie one with no more than five or six key result areas, each of which is expressed in one sentence. Get the participants to record their conclusions in the form set out in Table 10.1 (document 2).

5 Ask the participants to study the transcript and draw up objectives and key performance indicators for each of the key result areas and enter them in the second and third columns of the form.

6 Look at the results (or a sample if time is limited) and comment to the group on them (strengths and weaknesses). Do not refer in your comments to any individual. (10 minutes)

7 Ask the members of the group to comment on their experience. (10 minutes)

8 Summarize to the group the lessons learnt. Refer as necessary to the key result areas and objectives that have been produced for this role as set out in document 3. Only use this when it will help to give an example: it is better to distil one from the profiles produced by the group. (10 minutes)

Conducting the exercise

(Document 1 is shown overleaf; documents 2 and 3 are contained in Tables 10.1 and 10.2.)

Document 1: Transcript of a role analysis interview

The following is an edited transcript of an interview conducted by an analyst to provide the information required to prepare a role profile for a quality control technician in a food manufacturing company. The transcript refers to the main questions put by the analyst during the interview; the various supplementary questions have been omitted. The answers to the main questions are set out below.

Could you briefly summarize the main purpose of your job – what you are here to achieve?
I am responsible for the quality control of the four products on our cooked meats product line. I have to check that they meet our quality standards. I also check to ensure that we conform to food hygiene standards and regulations.

How do you do this?
As far as quality control is concerned, I have to know all about the specifications for each of the four products. This includes the basic ingredients, the mix of these ingredients, taste and smell, appearance and usability. I do this by conducting regular tests of a sample of products. I also check the labelling and packaging from time to time to ensure that these are in line with the specifications.

What sort of tests do you carry out?
Our quality control guide lays down the standard tests and sample sizes. There is a range of tests including microbiological and chemical tests. Some are quite complex; others, such as visual tests of appearance, are relatively straightforward. When it comes to tasting I have to use my judgement. I know what the product *should* taste like and I have to do my best to identify any difference significant enough to warrant action. We have tasting panels, which meet regularly to check on products. I organize the tasting panel for my products but this is a longer-term process the main purpose of which is to influence the product specification. However, I am the first line of defence and it is up to me to spot any immediate problems so that they can be put right.

What do you do about test results?

If there is a problem, I refer it initially to the product line manager so that she can deal with any issue over which she has control. I am expected to offer my opinion on what needs to be done if this is suggested by test results. If it is a more fundamental problem concerning such things as ingredients, the mix or production methods, the product line manager will refer them to product development. I am usually involved in explaining my findings there.

I submit regular (monthly) reports to the manager of the product line and to the quality control manager (my boss). My reports are also sent to the product development department. They summarize the results of the tests and highlight any issues that in my view need to be addressed. I am not expected to make recommendations on how the issue should be resolved, although my opinion is sometimes sought by manufacturing and product development. I also attend regular quality control meetings where I am expected to report on any issues and join in discussions.

What about the hygiene side of your responsibilities?

Although this does not take up as much time as my routine testing activities, this is a vital aspect of my work. I have to be fully aware of our own hygiene standards, which are rigorous. But I must also be completely au fait with the UK food regulations and, importantly, those within Europe (we export quite a lot to Europe). I also have to know a lot about methods of ensuring that the standards are maintained and what sort of actions can be taken to deal with any problems.

My job is to carry out hazard analyses at fixed stages of the production process – we call them 'critical control points'. I use a checklist to do this, but I am expected to delve into hygiene issues that are not specifically covered by the checklist. I have to know what I am looking for.

If I identify a hazard I report it immediately to the product line manager, explaining exactly what the problem is and making suggestions on what action should be taken. I am the expert on hygiene for the line. The action may involve stopping the production line, and in an emergency I have the authority to do that (that has never happened in my time here).

Do you have contacts with customers?

Not directly, but if a customer (a store or an individual) complains about one of my products, customer services ask me to investigate it and report to them on whether there is a problem and if so what. This may involve testing samples sent in by customers. It is up to customer services to decide how to deal with the complainer.

How do you know that you have done a good job?
Clearly, I will have done a good job if the tests and inspections I carry out are conducted thoroughly in accordance with the requirements of our quality control guide and by reference to hygiene regulations. I have to earn the respect of product line managers and the product development department as someone who knows what she is talking about and acts professionally.

My reports need to be clear, readable and submitted on time. My opinions on quality and hygiene must be evidence-based and I must be able to support my conclusions with that evidence.

I will have done a good job if I offer relevant and practical comments and suggestions to the product line manager, my boss and the product development department. I will also have done a good job if I respond promptly to requests from customer services to deal with customer complaints and provide them with the information they need to deal with the complaint.

Table 10.1   Document 2: Key result areas and objectives record

Role title:	
Overall purpose of role:	
Key result areas	**Objectives**

Table 10.2   Document 3: Example of completed key result areas and objectives record

Role title: Quality control technician

Overall purpose of role: To carry out quality control for the four products on the cooked meats product line

Key result areas	Objectives
1 Conduct tests to establish the extent to which a range of food products meets quality and food hygiene standards.	Tests and inspections are conducted thoroughly in accordance with the requirements of the quality control guide and by reference to hygiene regulations.
2 Prepare regular reports summarizing test results and findings.	Reports are clear, readable and submitted on time.
3 Provide advice to product line managers on actions to remedy quality or hygiene problems.	Advice on quality and hygiene is evidence-based and implemented; earns the respect of internal clients for professionalism.
4 Contribute to reviews of how quality and hygiene standards can be improved.	Relevant and practical comments and suggestions are made to product line managers and the product development department.
5 Prepare replies for customer services to send to customers who have complained about the quality of any item in the product range.	Respond promptly to requests from customer services to deal with customer complaints and provide them with the information they need to deal with the complaint.

Objective setting, Exercise 2

This exercise follows up Exercise 1 by providing an opportunity to prepare a role profile and a role's objectives from real life. It should be conducted as follows.

1 State the objectives of the exercise: *To provide participants with practice in preparing a 'real life' role profile listing key result areas and the associated objectives.*

2 Ask the group to split up into pairs.

3 Explain that in carrying out this exercise they should refer to their experience of completing Exercise 1.

4 Ask members of each pair to interview in turn the other member of the pair about his or her role (ie, A interviews B then B interviews A) and write up a basic role profile that includes definitions of the role's overall purpose, its key result areas (no more than five or six) and its objectives. (90 minutes)

5 Issue document 2 on which to record their conclusions on the overall purpose, key result areas and objectives of the role.

6 Look at the resulting role profiles (or a sample if time is limited) and comment to the group on the outcomes (strengths and weaknesses). Do not refer in your comments to any individual. (15 minutes)

7 Ask the members of the group to comment on their experience. (10 minutes)

8 Summarize the lessons learnt. (5 minutes)

WORKSHOP 4: HOW TO HANDLE CHALLENGING CONVERSATIONS

Presentation

1 Don't wait until a formal review meeting. Have a quiet word at the first sign that something is going wrong.

2 Get the facts in advance – what happened, when and why.

3 Plan the meeting on the basis of the facts and what is known about the individual. Define what is to be achieved.

4 Set the right tone from the start of the meeting – adopt a calm, measured, deliberate but friendly approach.

5 Begin the conversation by explaining the purpose of the meeting, indicating to the individual what the issue is and giving specific examples.

6 Focus on the issue and not the person.

7 Ask for an explanation. Ask unloaded questions to clarify the issues and explore them together.

8 Allow people to have their say and listen to them.

9 Keep an open mind and don't jump to conclusions.

10 Acknowledge the individual's position and any mitigating circumstances.

11 Ask the employee for proposals to resolve the situation, discuss the options and if possible agree on action by the individual, the manager or jointly.

12 If agreement cannot be reached, managers may have to define the way forward, with reasons – they are in charge!

Role play: A difficult conversation at Smith and Ledger

Brief for manager

You are Gerry Brown, a departmental manager at Smith and Ledger, an import/export business. Two months ago you asked one of your assistant managers for a report describing the information needs of the department. This was to be the first step in the process of enhancing the computer systems. You wanted a clear picture of what information was used, where it came from and how reliable it was. You also wanted the information classified by use (ie each job in the department was to be listed with its information needs). You appreciated that this was a complex task but were confident that your assistant manager could do it. The deadline was today and your assistant manager has e-mailed you to say that it hasn't been finished and should be ready in a fortnight. This annoys you because only two weeks ago when you asked if there were any problems you were told there were none.

You have to produce an overview of the department's requirements over the next five years. Your boss will speak to you next week and you are only waiting for your assistant manager's report to finish yours. You did emphasize its importance when you asked for it. You have asked your assistant manager to see you.

Brief for the assistant manager

You are Pat Fenwick, an assistant manager at Smith and Ledger, an import/export business. Two months ago your boss, the departmental manager, Gerry Brown, gave you a project to do. It was to record the information requirements of the department in terms of its use, sources and reliability. You were told that it was to contribute to something your manager was doing – a report for senior management on the future computer system needs of the department.

It was due to be finished today. It isn't. You have found it extremely boring and the help you have received from other members of the department is minimal. They don't want to know. In any case, every job you have examined (you have now finished them all) seems to have a very wide range of sources of information that the people who perform them assume you know about or forgot to mention. This is, presumably, because they are so familiar with it that it has become second nature. As a result it has taken much longer than you expected to gather the information required. You were asked by your boss last week how things were going and you said fine, even though they weren't, because you didn't think you could find a satisfactory explanation for the delay – the difficulties arising from complexity were real enough but you know in your heart of hearts that they could have been overcome with more effort on your part.

You have now sent your boss an e-mail saying that the report will be ready in a fortnight. The only thing you are bothered about is that, although you found the task tedious, you failed to tell your boss about your difficulties or ask for help, even when asked. If criticized, you will defend yourself up to the hilt on the grounds that you were given a difficult task over an impossible timescale which, against the odds, you have done your best to complete. You cannot imagine that a delay of only two weeks could be really serious.

You have now been summoned to see your manager. You assume it is about the report and, although you are aware that it is delayed, you are not in the mood to accept any harsh criticism.

WORKSHOP 5: COACHING SKILLS

Presentation

Coaching defined

Coaching is the ability to take the opportunities presented by the job itself and use them in a conscious manner to improve the knowledge, skills, competencies and therefore performance of the learner. It is fundamental to performance management and generally to good management practice.

How coaching works

Every time a manager delegates a new task to someone a coaching opportunity is created to help the individual learn any new skills or techniques needed to get the job done. Every time a manager provides feedback to an individual after a task has been completed there is an opportunity to help that individual do better next time.

Coaching as part of the normal process of management

Help people to develop new or improved skills (teaching/instructing):

- Discuss how to develop skills during feedback sessions or performance reviews.
- Use whatever situations that may arise as opportunities to promote learning, eg asking someone to carry out an unfamiliar task.
- Make people aware of how well they are performing.
- Practise controlled delegation.
- Encourage people to look at higher-level problems and how they would tackle them.

Approach to coaching

- Look for the best in people.
- Build on their strengths.
- Help people to help themselves.
- Encourage self-directed learning.
- Plan coaching as part of a development programme.

Coaching techniques

- Encourage people to think through issues.
- Get them to see things differently.
- Enable them to work out solutions for themselves which they can 'own'.
- Empower them to do things differently.

Instruction techniques

1 Present.

2 Demonstrate.

3 Practice.

The benefits of controlled delegation

- Delegation is an effective method of coaching.
- It is a natural part of what managers do and it provides a great opportunity for people to develop new skills or extend existing ones.
- The process of controlled delegation can indicate to managers where people need guidance and help.

Techniques of controlled delegation

To make the most of delegation, managers should ensure that individuals understand:

- Why the work needs to be done.
- What they are expected to do.
- How they are expected to do it.
- The date by which they are expected to do it.
- The authority they have to make decisions.
- The problems they must refer back.
- The progress or completion reports they should submit.
- How you propose to guide and monitor them.
- The resources and help they will have to complete the work.

Coaching through feedback

A feedback session as part of a performance and development conversation (a 'check-in') can be used as an opportunity for coaching when it involves:

- noting what has gone well so that a basis is provided for further development;
- identifying areas where performance outcomes show that there are aspects of knowledge and skills that should be developed;
- providing instant advice or guidance on what needs to be done;
- indicating any learning need that can be met by further coaching or other form of development.

Exercise 1: Giving instructions

1 State the objective: *To illustrate ways in which coaching can take place in the shape of helping people to learn a task or skill.*

2 Divide the whole group into pairs.

3 Ask each pair to think about a straightforward task they carry out or with which they are familiar, for example writing a report, making a presentation to colleagues, using PowerPoint to produce an animated slide, operating a simple machine, preparing a Gant Chart or baking a cake.

4 Ask them to decide how they would instruct someone in this task.

5 Tell the members of each pair to take it in turns to practise giving the instruction to the other member of the pair.

6 Ask the receiver of the instruction to assess the quality of the instruction.

7 Lead a general discussion on the lessons learnt.

Exercise 2: Coaching through delegation

The objective of this exercise is to increase understanding of the use of controlled delegation as a means of coaching. It is conducted by asking workshop participants to look at each of the delegation scenarios shown in Table 10.3 and decide which of the alternative approaches to dealing with the situation they prefer and why. This is followed by a general discussion on what can be learnt from this exercise.

Table 10.3 Delegation scenarios

Delegation scenario	Consider the advantages and disadvantages of the alternative approaches
1 You are conscious of the fact that you are working too hard and going into too much detail and therefore need to delegate more, but you do not feel that your team members are able to take on more responsibility because they lack the necessary skills. What should you do?	a Get the Learning and Development department to carry out a skills analysis and organize a training course for the whole group to fill any gaps. b Take each member of the group in turn and ensure that they acquire the skills they need through a specially selected training course. c Weigh up the pros and cons of controlled delegation or direct instruction and act accordingly. d Select the more able members of your team and give them more responsibility on the assumption that they will be able to learn the skills required from you or their colleagues.
2 One of your departmental managers is clearly under stress and has fallen down on one or two jobs recently. Following a feedback discussion you come to the conclusion that he is trying to do too much himself. During the discussion it emerges that the reason for this is that he does not trust his team members to do the work. What should you do next?	a Tell him that he must delegate more. b Ask him to think of any ways in which he could delegate more. c Ask him to consider what he could do to enhance the skills of his staff and therefore put himself in a position in which he would be happier to delegate more. d Sit down with him and discuss how the skills of each member of his staff could be enhanced.

Delegation scenario	Consider the advantages and disadvantages of the alternative approaches
3 A member of your team is not doing well because, while she carries out most of her tasks satisfactorily, she performs a group of what are perhaps the key tasks badly. As far as you can tell this is because she has not had the opportunity to develop the knowledge or skills required. What steps should you take?	**a** Send her on a course. **b** Sit down with her and tell her how to do it. **c** Get someone else to sit down with her and tell her how to do it. **d** Select tasks from the group of tasks in which she has problems and get her to carry out specific assignments with guidance and help as required from yourself.
4 You are considering ways in which you can improve the performance of your department by developing the skills and knowledge of your staff. The work of your department is quite varied. It involves the collection and analysis of complex data, providing advice to line managers on the implications of the analyses, and producing reports to senior management on the outcome of surveys and reviews and the actions that may be required. There are a number of alternative ways of doing this as listed in the opposite box and you want to consider the advantages and disadvantages of each method.	**a** Formal off-the-job training courses. **b** Planned experience. **c** Individual instruction/coaching. **d** Controlled delegation.

Less formal learning

Formal training programmes are useful but not enough. Performance management skills are best developed through coaching and mentoring, which can be supplemented by e-learning programmes. The HR department can play an important role in organizing these learning activities but it is best to use experienced line managers as coaches and mentors.

Conclusions

- Performance management does not work when managers don't believe it's worth doing or, even when they do, lack the skills to do it properly. Employees also need to know why performance management is important, and they require training in goal setting, using feedback and development planning.

- Formal learning programmes can attempt to cover all aspects of performance management in two days or at least a day. Less than two days may only provide sufficient space to cover the basic features of performance management with little time left to practise skills – an essential element in training. Half a day is wholly inadequate.

- Learning, especially skills development, is best achieved by participative methods – guided discussions, role plays and other exercises.

Reference

e-reward (2014) *Survey of Performance Management*, e-reward, Stockport

Reinventing performance management

Introduction

The evidence suggests that traditional performance management is broken. It is too often an expensive, complex system for making people unhappy.

The common thread running through the examples in Chapter 4 and the Appendices is disillusion with the relevance and effectiveness of formal performance reviews and their replacement with more frequent and less formal performance and development conversations between managers and individuals. Traditional overall ratings were abolished in five of the six cases. In one organization (Microsoft) typically complex methods of objective setting have been replaced by a much simpler approach involving the agreement of priorities. Performance pay decisions have been decoupled from performance reviews.

In this concluding chapter the themes as presented in earlier chapters are brought together to produce a coherent picture of what needs to be done about performance management. In effect, what is proposed here is that performance management should be reinvented. The chapter starts with a description of the main areas in which the process of reinvention can take place as suggested by an analysis of current trends in major organizations. It continues with an examination of how a reinvention programme can be managed.

Areas for reinvention

The areas for reinvention considered in more detail below are:

- Re-examination of the process of objective setting, possibly involving the replacement of complex traditional 'SMART' procedures with processes for deciding on priorities.
- Replacement of the formal annual or twice-yearly performance review with more frequent and less formal performance and development conversations.
- Abolition of overall rating and forced ranking systems.
- Decoupling decisions on performance pay from performance reviews.
- More sustained focus on development rather than 'managing' performance.

In each case the emphasis is on simplicity: removing complex and jargon-ridden methodology and making the process of reviewing performance easier for managers and employees alike.

Objective setting

Complex objective-setting procedures involving, for example, the requirement for 'SMART' objectives, key result areas and key performance indicators should be replaced with a system based simply on determining and agreeing a limited number of key priorities. The priorities can include targets and delivery timescales as appropriate and will indicate how the extent to which they have been met can be assessed.

A process of deciding on a limited number of priorities is simpler and easier to understand and operate. Managers often feel that they have better things to do than draw up lists of key result areas and performance indicators and may find it difficult to meet artificial SMART objective criteria.

Replace the annual performance review

The formal annual or twice-yearly performance review or appraisal has been subject to much criticism. The fundamental problem is that getting managers to conduct a formal performance review once or twice a year creates the impression that the management of someone's performance can be accomplished in the hour or so that it takes to conduct what can easily be an unsatisfactory experience for both parties. What happens during the rest of the year does not matter.

A yearly or half-yearly meeting means that insufficient attention may be given to what happened some time ago and assessments will be subjected to the 'recency' effect, ie focusing on recent events rather than looking at the whole picture. Furthermore, waiting for six or twelve months before setting new objectives is unrealistic in today's fast-moving conditions.

Taking part in a traditional formal performance review can be a daunting and therefore dreaded occasion for both parties. Conducting satisfactory reviews needs considerable and unusual skill. The requirements for a successful meeting are demanding, and there is the multiplicity of purposes, including improving performance, developing skills, spotting potential, identifying poor performers and informing performance pay decisions. These cannot be satisfied in one brief meeting. Lisa Dodge, Director, Global Performance Programmes at Microsoft, said that its previous approach tried to do too many things. In a vivid phrase she observed that: 'It was like a Swiss army knife of performance management – we were using it for everything from allocating reward to categorizing talent.'

It is hardly surprising that many managers and indeed employees generally find it difficult. They cannot be blamed for paying lip-service to something they cannot comprehend and find daunting and just about impossible to do well. As a result meetings can be superficial, inconclusive and even demotivating. It can only work if the purposes are simplified and there is mutual trust and understanding between the perceptions of both parties. Otherwise hostility and resistance are likely to emerge.

Traditional performance reviews should be replaced by a process that recognizes what should be obvious – that managing performance is something that happens throughout the year, not just at infrequent intervals. More frequent get-togethers of managers with individual members of their team are required. These should take the form of a conversation rather than a formal review and can therefore be called 'performance and development conversations' (PDCs). They include feedback from the manager and, possibly, some self-assessment by the individual. They focus on the priorities people set for themselves and the progress they are making on meeting those priorities and contributing to the performance of their team and the organization. They include discussions on immediate and longer-term development needs.

Rating

The disadvantages of rating considerably outweigh the advantages. As Lisa Dodge of Microsoft explained: 'Our employees don't need ratings to know how they are doing... We want rich conversations rather than assuming an employee's performance can be boiled down to a simple label.' Buckingham and Goodall (2015) commented: 'In the end, it's not the particular number we assign to a person that's the problem; rather, it's the fact that there *is* a single number.'

Ratings should therefore be abandoned. They would not be generated by performance and development conversations (PDCs) and so could focus on the future, agreeing priorities and development needs and the actions required to satisfy them. The abolition of ratings would also involve ending the pernicious practice of forced ranking.

There are perfectly effective methods of deciding on performance pay increases without the use of crude overall ratings. Similarly, there are good ways of identifying potential in the absence of overall ratings. For example, Deloitte, as reported by Buckingham and Goodall (2015), asks team leaders to respond to the following four future-focused statements about each of their team members:

1 Given what I know of this person's performance, and if it were my money, I would award this person the highest possible compensation increase and bonus.

2 Given what I know of this person's performance, I would always want him or her on my team.

3 This person is at risk for low performance.

4 This person is ready for promotion today.

In effect, team leaders are asked what they would *do* with each team member rather than what they *think* of that individual.

Decoupling performance pay decisions

Focusing on performance management as a means of deciding on pay awards may conflict with the developmental purposes of performance management. This will particularly be the case if ratings are used – the performance review meeting will concentrate on the ratings that emerge from it and how much money will be forthcoming. Issues concerning development and non-financial reward approaches will be subordinated to this preoccupation with pay. The problem of reconciling the developmental aspects of performance management or appraisal and pay has been with us for decades. I commented as long ago as 1976 that:

> It is undesirable to have a direct link between the performance review and the reward review. The former must aim primarily at improving performance and, possibly, assessing potential. If this is confused with a salary review, everyone becomes over-concerned about the impact of the assessment on the increment... It is better to separate the two.
>
> (Armstrong, 1976)

Many organizations are now attempting to get over this problem by holding development and pay review meetings on separate dates, often several months apart (decoupling).

Focus on employee development

Employee development is a prime objective, on the basis of assessing the 'how' as well as the 'what' and establishing and satisfying development needs as they arise.

The reinvention programme

The reinvention programme should start with an analysis of the present arrangements. This will lead to an assessment of the possible areas for action taking into account the advantages and disadvantages of the alternatives in the context of the organization's situation and requirements. The programme should include discussions with managers and other employees on their views about current arrangements and their thoughts on future developments. Formats for this assessment of views and analysis of options are set out in Tables 11.1 and 11.2.

Table 11.1 Performance management survey

Rate the extent to which you agree or disagree with the following statements about how performance functions in this organization on a scale of 1–5 where:	
1 = fully agree, 2 = agree, 3 = not sure, 4 = disagree, 5 = strongly disagree	
1 Performance management is perceived by top management as a key process for managing the business	1 2 3 4 5
2 Line managers are committed to performance management	1 2 3 4 5
3 Line managers have the skills to manage performance effectively	1 2 3 4 5
4 Performance management processes are clear, simple and easily understood by all concerned	1 2 3 4 5
5 Clear, demanding but achievable work objectives or priorities are agreed by managers and their team members	1 2 3 4 5
6 Performance management is concerned not only with *what* people achieve but also *how* they achieve it	1 2 3 4 5
7 The performance management system helps managers to manage more effectively	1 2 3 4 5
8 Performance management makes a positive impact on individual performance	1 2 3 4 5
9 I look forward to performance review sessions	1 2 3 4 5
10 Helpful performance and development conversations with useful feedback are held at frequent intervals during the year	1 2 3 4 5
11 Managers take their coaching and employee development responsibilities seriously	1 2 3 4 5
12 I believe that performance management is a waste of time	1 2 3 4 5

Table 11.2 Analysis of possible new arrangements

Possible new arrangement	Advantages	Disadvantages	Action
OBJECTIVE-SETTING			
Replace complex objective-setting procedures involving, for example, the requirement for 'SMART' objectives, key result areas and key performance indicators, with a system based simply on determining and agreeing a limited number of key priorities. The priorities can include targets and delivery timescales as appropriate and will indicate how the extent to which they have been met can be assessed.	The process is simpler and easier to understand and operate. Managers can feel that they have better things to do than draw up lists of key result areas and performance indicators and may find it difficult to meet the SMART objective criteria.	Abandoning the discipline of setting SMART objectives related to rigorous definitions of key result areas and performance indicators may result in a vacuum that will not be filled by the vaguer concept of priorities. This may fail to provide people with adequate information about job requirements and leave them with insufficient direction.	
ANNUAL PERFORMANCE REVIEW			
Replace the annual performance review with more frequent 'performance and development conversations' that provide informal feedback and include the discussion and revision of priorities and development plans.	Gets rid of the 'dishonest annual ritual' of the yearly formal performance review and appraisal session, which is often dreaded by both managers and individuals and, if done at all, is carried out perfunctorily. This is replaced by much less formal conversations that arise naturally out of the normal process of work.	Abolishing the annual review means that there will no longer be an opportunity to hold what can be a 'stock-taking' exercise that provides a defined framework for development planning and objective setting.	

Table 11.2 Analysis of possible new arrangements (continued)

Possible new arrangement	Advantages	Disadvantages	Action
RATINGS			
Abolish ratings	Overcomes the fundamental objections to rating performance, ie that ratings are largely subjective and it is difficult to achieve consistency between the ratings given by different managers. Even if objectivity is achieved, to sum up the total performance of a person with a single rating is a gross over-simplification of what may be a complex set of factors influencing that performance. To label people as 'average' or 'below average', or whatever equivalent terms are used, is both demeaning and demotivating.	Abolishing ratings would mean that the following advantages would disappear: • they provide a convenient means of summing up judgements; • they motivate people by giving them something to strive for in the shape of higher ratings; • they provide a basis for identifying potential. It can also be argued that it is impossible to have performance pay without rating, but there are ways of overcoming this.	
FORCED RANKING			
Abolish forced ranking	Get rid of the climate of fear and the likelihood that those ranked highest on the scale are more competitive and less cooperative than those ranked lower.	No longer possible to use forced ranking as a means of identifying those employees who should be dismissed for poor performance.	

LINK WITH PERFORMANCE PAY

Decouple performance pay decisions from performance reviews

Avoids the conflict between focusing on performance management as a means of pay and satisfying the developmental purposes of performance management.

Makes the process more complex.

EMPLOYEE DEVELOPMENT

Emphasize employee development as a prime objective on the basis of assessing the 'how' as well as the 'what'. Rechristen performance management as 'performance and development'.

Focus on the positive aspects of developing skills and abilities that improve performance and further careers.

None.

The employee survey in Table 11.1 can be used to assess the effectiveness of the present performance management arrangements by obtaining views on the extent to which there is agreement or disagreement with a number of statements about how it functions. Use Table 11.2 as the basis for analysing possible new arrangements.

Approach to reinvention

The approach adopted to reinventing performance management has to recognize the problems involved in meeting possibly demanding objectives and overcoming the practical and political difficulties that will occur. Following their research, Strebler *et al* (2001) wrote about this as follows.

> Personnel management textbooks are full of touching accounts of how to design and implement performance appraisal and management schemes in organizations. The models they propose are based on a rational and linear logic, which assumes that an organization's goals can be translated into individual goals, which, in turn, can be delivered through feedback, training, development and reward. The reality of organizational life is somewhat different.

The following practical advice on the dos and don'ts of introducing performance management or making substantial changes to an existing scheme was given by the respondents to the e-reward survey (2014).

Do:

> 'Work out why the organization wants to have a performance management system. If the decision is to introduce or change the performance management system then make sure that the way it works reflects the organization culture. Integrate the performance management system with other HR information systems.'

> 'Gain the support of senior people in the organization. Do a lot of prep work including consultation with staff and managers to find out what kind of performance management system would work in

this particular environment. Once agreed, really invest in regular training and revision of how the process works.'

'Think about what you want from any performance management approach – why have it at all? Listen to feedback from your business owners/shareholders, senior management and staff/employee representatives, decide on the things that will make a difference to your business in the next five years and design your solution to meet that need. Remember, designing a system which picks out the best and worst can ignore the majority who become disenfranchised with performance management. Design it to engage the majority as this creates value.'

'Spend most time on consulting/communicating, particularly with the managers expected to do it, rather than on a clever "design".'

'Keep it simple and easy to understand. If changing an existing scheme, review what is wrong with the current system before designing a new one. Time may be better spent embedding the existing one than changing it. Ensure the system is backed up with regular performance discussions, not just a discussion once or twice a year.'

'Involve line managers in the design phase, asking what works and doesn't. Keep it simple. Explain the process to the whole workforce. Let line managers own the process.'

'Get senior management to support you, otherwise it won't work. All the effort will be wasted. The biggest success factor is based on how it's rolled out.'

'Get senior management buy in to the process as any change needs to be driven from the top. Design your system through employee focus groups as they will tell you what they like and don't like about it. Use the feedback to improve the system. The employee focus group staff are more likely to champion the system as they have been instrumental in developing it, which helps with engagement.'

'Consistency – one scheme for all, make it about good conversations, not just a process.'

'Be clear about what you are trying to achieve and how you will measure/evaluate whether you have achieved the aims. Have clear strategies and processes for dealing with poor performance and ensure managers are trained in how to deal with poor performance. Create a climate where implementing performance management systems is an absolutely necessary part of a manager's role and a real requirement of the job.'

'Assess what are the objectives/priorities for your organization. Do some benchmarking and best practice but always link back to what will work for your organization right now. Review the process: what was right a few years ago may now need changing.'

Don't:

'View performance management as an annual task such as appraisals; view it as a daily part of operations. Don't use appraisals as a means of dealing with performance issues, tackle them as soon as they become apparent through use of performance improvement plans for example, or if it is a conduct issue adopt a different line.'

'Use the process to emphasize the past. If you cannot pay much then do not use money as a key motivator.'

'Underestimate the role of middle and line managers – they are the ones that will make or break your performance management process. Don't assume that because the goals and benefits of the scheme are clear to you, they will be understood, agreed and considered a priority by others. Don't forget that no matter what, the user interface of your performance management system must be ridiculously easy to understand – even if the concepts behind it are not.'

'Try to do too much too soon – evaluate the culture of the business and ask if it's ready for the changes that you want to implement.'

'Think you will not have anomalies in trying to link pay and performance. Don't think line managers will have this on the top of their to-do list unless there is either some pain or gain.'

'Think that a clever system is best.'

'Spend a lot of time designing forms and scoring systems.'

'Presume information is cascaded by managers.'

'Believe that performance management systems will please everyone – it's not possible.'

'Overcomplicate things by looking at 23 or 32 competencies.'

'Overcomplicate – it isn't necessary, don't do it for the sake of it, don't force people down an over-engineered process. If they set aligned objectives and have the skills to review these as well as the skills for challenging conversations – this is performance management!'

'Make the process too cumbersome with too many steps; if managers have too many evaluations to prepare, too many to validate, quality will be lost.'

'Make the appraisal such a big event; it should be part of a continuous process of coaching and feedback… increasingly thinking that the performance conversation should be de-linked from pay increase as it distorts the thinking.'

'Link the performance management directly to incentive pay. The focus switches from assessing employees – and getting the best out of them – to having an incentive pay figure in mind for an employee and using the performance management system to secure the incentive pay figure.'

'Let it become a box-ticking exercise, to be completed once or twice a year and then forgotten about. Don't let it be a negative experience for all involved, which might be overly bureaucratic and time-consuming, or punitive in nature.'

Finally…

There are issues in performance management over rating and setting objectives, but perhaps the most fundamental one is the annual performance review. Here is what three managers told Dilys Robinson of the Institute for Employment Studies (2013) about how they managed performance:

'So, the key for me is just one-to-one time, and they know what they're aiming for, and we talk about it regularly. So it never really gets to the situation where there's like a really great big formal sit-down to say let's review everything you've done.'

'I think it's regular dialogue... at least once a fortnight for an extended period of time, just one to one and just about them and the work they're doing and what's going on... just so that I understand what they're doing and so I can give a bit of a steer or give them a bit of coaching if they need some coaching; help them if they want some help and support.'

'Every week I have a one-to-one session with people who work for me. And it's half an hour; it's the opportunity to talk things over with people. I say to people it's your time with me. But, to be honest, it's not just that; it's me getting to talk to them.'

Perhaps the best way to deal with the annual performance review issue, indeed the whole problem of making performance management work, is to get managers to act like this rather than compel them to conform to the bureaucratic requirements of a typical performance management system. These managers are managing performance not operating a system. The way ahead is therefore to select, develop, encourage and support managers to do just that.

References

Armstrong, M (1976) *A Handbook of Personnel Management Practice*, Kogan Page, London

Buckingham, M and Goodall, A (2015) Reinventing performance management, *Harvard Business Review*, April, pp 40–50

e-reward (2014) *Survey of Performance Management Practice*, e-reward, Stockport

Robinson, D (2013) *The Engaging Manager and Sticky Situations*, Engaging Manager Report Series 493, Institute for Employment Studies, Brighton, www.employment–studies.co.uk/system/files/resources/files/493.pdf (accessed 17 October 2016)

Strebler, M T, Bevan, S and Robertson, D (2001) *Performance Review: Balancing objectives and content*, Institute for Employment Studies, Brighton

Appendix A

Performance management case study: Gap Inc

Introduction

In 2014, Gap launched a new performance management process: 'Grow. Perform. Succeed. (GPS)' for its headquarters' employees worldwide. The company is also introducing a slightly modified version of GPS for its retail store and distribution centre staff. As Rob Ollander-Krane, Senior Director, Organization Performance Effectiveness at Gap, who devised the new scheme, commented: 'We really wanted to drive performance and engage our employees and I don't think that a once a year, mostly administrative process that's tied to a fixed distribution curve can do that.' Gone are the formal reviews and performance ratings of the past; instead, managers and employees are encouraged to have 12 informal, undocumented conversations (called 'touch-base' meetings) about performance over the course of the year. Gap believes that GPS has 'repurposed' thousands of working hours and millions of dollars from tasks that did not drive performance to discussions that do. What's more, staff surveys suggest employees feel that the new process provides them with better feedback, offers more opportunities to learn and drives them to higher levels of performance.

The previous process

Gap used to have a 'traditional' performance management process – with goals set at the beginning of the year, a single end-of-year review meeting and performance ratings. As Rob Ollander-Krane observed:

> At the start of the year goals were set at the business level and then loosely cascaded down to business units, teams and individuals. Most people documented their personal goals somewhere, but many didn't. And most of those who did just put them in a drawer and didn't look at them again for 12 months, when they would write a 14-page tome to try and justify a better rating at their end-of-year review.

The ratings process was directly linked to the Gap bonus scheme, with higher grades leading to bigger pay-outs. Ollander-Krane said that:

> The way the process was set up, I think most employees saw the end-of-year performance discussion – which sometimes captured information that was 15 months old – as something they had to suffer through in order to get to their rating and find out how much money they were going to get. All they really wanted to know was, 'Did I get the A or the B grade and therefore I felt good, or did I get the C and it was just another lousy year?' Although the manager and employee discussed the content of the review, they weren't really having a conversation that drove performance – it was just what they had to do to get to the conversation about the money.

Not only did the process's structure distract from actually discussing performance, it sometimes led to further difficult conversations when managers' ratings were changed to fit the company's forced distribution curve. Ollander-Krane stated that:

> We used a curve to ensure our total bonus payments stayed within the overall budget, so we would sometimes have to revise our managers' ratings down... So leaders or HR would end up having contentious conversations with managers about changing their grades, and then the managers would have contentious conversations with their employees

when they had to go back and say, 'I know I said you were an A, but you're really a B'.

Above all else, the process was simply not delivering results in terms of improved business performance for Gap. It was complex, time-consuming and expensive. At the company's headquarters alone, it was estimated that people were spending 130,000 hours a year and significant payroll on performance management. And both managers and employees disliked it. As one employee complained in an opinion survey: 'I think the annual review and rating is a waste of an employee's time... causes unnecessary stress... and is really an old way of thinking in this modern day and age.' All of this, combined with a growing consensus among thought leaders in the HR and performance field that 'traditional' performance management had had its day, led Gap to decide the time had come to radically overhaul its approach.

Five objectives for the new scheme

To start the overhaul process, Ollander-Krane interviewed Gap's senior leaders on the behaviours that they were looking for to be more competitive in the marketplace. Through these discussions he created the following five objectives for the new performance management scheme:

1 Raise the bar of performance.
2 Provide meaningful reward for exceeding plan and consequences for missing.
3 Ensure managers take accountability for assessing, developing and rewarding performance.
4 Support a shift in culture from nice to nice *and* honest.
5 Be simple.

'All of their objectives made a lot of sense,' said Ollander-Krane:

Our previous scheme rewarded fairly average performance, so there was a need to raise the bar. And as half an employee's bonus was paid out even if the company was not performing, there was limited consequence for individuals if business was poor. Traditional performance management effectively handcuffs managers by telling them they can only talk to their employees once a year, while ratings force them to put employees into a fixed number of categories – we wanted managers to be more accountable for regularly assessing performance. We also wanted people to not be afraid to tell the truth and have 'real' conversations. And finally, we just wanted to make it as simple as possible – performance management doesn't have to be complicated.

A year-long journey

It took Ollander-Krane and his colleagues the whole of 2013 to develop the new performance management framework. The first four months were spent doing nothing but fact gathering and carrying out research:

> I read books, went to conferences and spoke to other companies that had reinvented the way they managed performance. I talked with thought leaders about their theories on how best to drive and motivate performance. I asked our employees what issues they had with the existing performance management process. And I met with our senior leaders to ask what additional behaviours they wanted to see from our employees in order to be competitive. It was incredibly eye-opening – it made me realize we'd been addressing performance management in all the wrong ways.

In particular, Ollander-Krane was influenced by the work of Stanford University psychologist Dr Carol Dweck and her concept of 'growth mind-set'. He explained:

> She believes that someone's intelligence is not innate or fixed at birth but that it can be developed – it's something that you can change and grow. Having a growth mind-set encourages people to embrace challenges, persist in the face of setbacks, see effort as the path to mastery, learn from feedback and find inspiration in others' success. And we used this as the philosophy for everything we did when designing the new approach.

Following the research stage, a team of people from all of the sub-functions within HR was assembled – including communications, employee relations, learning and development, talent management, legal, the goal-setting team and HR operations – to design and develop the new approach. 'We met for an hour once a week for a few months, working out what the new process could look like,' Ollander-Krane recalled. 'Then later on we had a two-day brainstorming session led by an external company to help us lay out our final plans and brand the new process.' He continued:

> We also invited one or two directors from each of the business units to form a senior advisory group that we could talk to about our philosophies and the programme elements we were creating and get their feedback – we even asked them to pilot some of our ideas with their employees.

> So we did a lot of work in the middle of the year getting people on board with what we were doing and making sure each of the business units was willing to go down this road with us – and 'course correcting' when necessary. Then as we got towards the end of the year we scheduled two important meetings to announce our final plans to senior leaders: one with our group of VPs and above in November, and then one with our directors and above in December.

Branding the new scheme

As well as getting the content and processes of the new scheme right, Ollander-Krane was also keen to ensure it had a name and brand that would engage employees. 'The previous scheme was called "Focal", which is a compensation term that meant nothing to our employees. With the new scheme we wanted something that would resonate in our culture.' The team settled on the name: Grow. Perform. Succeed. (GPS). As Ollander-Krane remarked:

> The name captures what we are trying to achieve – we want our employees to grow and for the focus to be on performance rather than management. But the initials – GPS – also match our stock name, so the name of our internal measure of performance now matches our external measure of performance... But what I really love about the name GPS is that it's an analogy for what we want our managers to do. A GPS

system in your car lets you set your destination, and then if you make a wrong turn as you're driving it recalculates in real time and gets you back on the right path. If a GPS in your car waited until you got to your destination to tell you you'd made a wrong turn, you'd never get there. But that's what traditional performance management does: it waits until you get to the destination – the end of the year – before telling you that you made a mistake. We wanted managers to be like a real GPS, course-correcting their employees' performance throughout the year.

The new GPS scheme

The GPS scheme has four main components:

1 A performance standard.
2 Goals.
3 Touch-bases.
4 Rewards.

1 A new performance standard

The scheme revolves around a newly developed performance stand-ard, which sets out the behaviours to which all Gap's managers and employees should aspire and against which they will be evaluated. It states:

> We set tough objectives and work hard to exceed our goals. We do what it takes to win in the marketplace with integrity. We live the values of our company. If we fall short of hitting our goals we quickly learn from our experience and strive to win. Managers inspire and drive perfor-mance of their teams through regular coaching and feedback.

'The performance standard essentially replaced our ratings scale, instead giving a broad overview of the behaviours we expect to see,' said Ollander-Krane. 'And it embodies every aspect of our new approach – having a growth mind-set, delivering and learning from feedback, and just having regular, open and honest conversations.' Significantly, it puts the focus as much on the 'how' you have achieved your goals as on the 'what' you have done.

2 A more personal goal-setting process

With the GPS approach, the company modified its previous goal-setting process. First, employees are only allowed a maximum of eight goals. Under the old process employees would end up with a long laundry list of tasks. Many had 20 or 30 things they were supposed to accomplish each year – it was like a job description. The new scheme allows them to focus on a much smaller number of important objectives.

Second, these goals should be outcomes rather than tasks. 'Driving performance is not about ticking off all the things you have on your "to do" list – it's about thinking about how the world will be different if you achieve them all,' said Ollander-Krane.

Ollander-Krane and his team created a 20-minute training module to help people understand this distinction between task-based goals and outcome-based goals, complete with examples of each. For example, a task-based goal might be: 'Send 200 e-mails per customer this year.' This offers no clarity on the business outcome the employee is trying to achieve – and if sending 200 e-mails does not result in a business outcome, you cannot say the employee has been successful.

In contrast, an outcome-based goal – for example: 'Increase online-initiated Gap sales revenue this year by x amount' – offers a clear outcome against which performance can be evaluated. But more important, it allows employees to determine the best way to accomplish the outcome – it does not lock them into one approach that might not be successful. Instead, they can try multiple approaches to achieve the goal.

'Third, we cascaded three enterprise-wide goals that were established by the senior leadership team. If an employee's work happens to align with one of these three goals then that's great. We try wherever possible to make these connections, but it's not always possible,' says Ollander-Krane:

> What's more important to us is that the employee and manager agree on the employee's goals. How they get there is up to them – we're expecting that the manager knows the three enterprise-wide goals and what their business unit goals are and that they help the employees make sure

their goals align with those. But ultimately, as long as there is agreement between the employee and manager, that is the most important part.

Goals are no longer wedded to an annual timeframe. Because the old process had an annual cycle of setting and evaluating goals, most employees set goals that were based on a 12-month cycle. 'We can be much more flexible under the new process,' said Ollander-Krane. 'My goals are three years long, for example, because that's how long we think it will take to make the behavioural changes we're seeking through the new performance management process. Others have goals that are just two or three months in length.'

Finally, goals are the only thing that is documented in GPS:

> We ask employees to write down their goals and keep them updated throughout the year. But we don't ask them to keep any record of their progress or to collect any evidence of whether they have achieved their goals. And they are supposed to be dynamic and change throughout the year, to ensure they are still relevant.

The only exception is for employees whose poor level of performance requires corrective action – this process is highly documented. Detailed records are kept of all conversations and agreed actions.

3 Monthly 'touch-base' meetings

Perhaps the biggest departure from the previous performance management process is the introduction of 12 'touch-base' sessions to replace the single year-end review meeting. These are intended to be informal discussions between managers and employees that can take place anywhere and at any time. None of these conversations is recorded. Ollander-Krane said:

> In the long term what we'd really love is for these conversations to take place any time they are needed. We don't really want to put a number on it or to say that they have to take place at certain times during the year – if an employee or a manager wants to talk about performance at any time, they should be able to do it. But we didn't want it to be completely freeform, at least in the first couple of years. So we have said employees should talk to their managers once a month. But where those

meetings happen is up to them – it could be over lunch, by the vending machine or even just while walking between meetings. And they can last anywhere from a few minutes to over an hour. But eventually we want to get to a point where these 'touch-bases' just happen as and when they are needed.

The meetings may be used to discuss any aspect of performance, although ideally employees should revisit their goals to make sure they are still relevant and to see if there are any new objectives that need to be added or current goals that need to be taken away. They should also discuss their performance against the new performance standard. Are they learning from their successes and failure? Are they demonstrating the values of the company? 'They might also talk about their key working relationships and their career aspirations,' says Ollander-Krane. 'The idea is to focus on these larger topics, rather than the day-to-day aspects of work.'

To help managers make the most of these discussions, Ollander-Krane developed a three-hour training module on how to give effective feedback during these conversations. It helps managers understand why giving and getting feedback can feel threatening and it teaches a model that already existed within Gap that encourages managers to ask employees three questions when giving feedback:

- What went well?
- Where did you get stuck?
- What would you do differently next time?

'Using this simple model every time you talk to employees helps create more certainty for them – they know what to expect,' says Ollander-Krane. 'But it also helps build their autonomy and helps them feel part of the team – and it facilitates a real two-way conversation rather than just forcing the employee to listen to what the manager has to say.'

4 Changes to reward

The relationship between performance and reward has been revolutionized under GPS. With no ratings – and no forced distribution curve – managers have had to rethink how they allocate merit and bonus payments to their employees, while the composition of the bonus itself has been changed to place more of a focus on company performance. The rewards conversation has also been completely separated from the performance conversation.

The bonus scheme at Gap accounts for a significant part of take-home pay. Under the old arrangement, 50 per cent of an employee's bonus pay-out was based on company performance and 50 per cent was based on individual performance. 'This meant that if your manager gave you an A, B or C in a year when the company didn't hit its financial targets, you would still get some money,' says Ollander-Krane.

If you were awarded a B grade your target pay-out would be 1.5 times the C pay-out. And if you got an A grade, your target pay-out would be two times the C pay-out. 'So it added a lot of weight to the managers' decisions about employee ratings and it created quite a competitive environment around the year-end review – employees would really push their managers hard to try and get a higher rating.'

Under GPS, however, the structure of the bonus scheme has changed. 'We didn't think the 50/50 split was needed any more,' says Ollander-Krane:

> It was introduced in different times, when the company was going through a tough period and we wanted to hold on to our talent while we turned the ship around. And it was a generous programme – more generous than our competition. So we wanted to tie the whole programme much more closely to business performance.

There was even some discussion with the senior leadership team about whether to move to a scheme that was based 100 per cent on company performance, with no individual element at all. But in the end they decided to move to a 75/25 set up – with 75 per cent of the pay-out determined by the business's financial results and the remaining 25 per cent based on individual performance. Although even here, the size of the individual pay-out is now dictated by business performance – if certain targets aren't hit, even a high performing employee may not receive a bonus or it will be considerably smaller, which makes sense. But it doesn't mean employees can't make the same or even more money than before – if the business in on fire and you are on fire, you'll make more money. But the overall idea is that if the business makes money, you'll make money.

Ollander-Krane added: 'Forget anything else we did with performance management – this change alone was probably the most significant in terms of changing employee thinking. They knew something was different – that they had to work harder and the business had to perform better if they wanted more money in their pockets.'

No more ratings

With the removal of ratings, employees are no longer awarded a grade at the end of the year. But managers are required to differentiate employee performance in some way. 'They are not giving an A, B or C, but they still need to rank their employees,' says Ollander-Krane:

> They still need to say here's my number one employee, here's my number two, here's my number three – and to allocate their merit and bonus pot accordingly. But they are not trying to force people into categories. It's a much simpler exercise – and much more similar to the way we expect our managers to manage our products. When a product sells well, you reinvest in it – and the concept here is the same: you give more money to the person who is delivering the best results. It feels like a much more intuitive process.

A pre-calibration discussion

In addition to trying to make a stronger connection between business performance and rewards, Gap wanted to get rid of the pain associated with the calibration discussions that sometimes ended with a manager having to change the rating they had assigned to the employee's performance. 'To do so, we moved calibration forward from after the performance discussion to before,' says Ollander-Krane:

> We now have a pre-calibration discussion to set each manager's bonus budget ahead of their end-of-year reward conversations with employees – so they know exactly how much money they have to allocate across

their team. And we also give managers a description of what our senior leaders think 'amazing' performance looked like that year. Once they have these two things, they should know exactly how much to award each member of their team.

Finally, in a move that symbolizes the company's new approach to performance management, the reward discussion now takes place separately to any discussion of performance:

> Instead of having one lengthy conversation at the end of the year that tried to cover performance and reward, we now have 12 performance conversations throughout the year and one brief rewards conversation at the end of the year. Basically, all the manager needs to say is 'Here's how the company did, here's how our business unit did, here's a reminder of a couple of things you did really well and a couple of places where you are still developing – now here's your money.' And if managers have done their job, regularly discussing performance during the year, there should be no surprises or lack of alignment. Compared to the lengthy and sometimes contentious conversations they used to have, it should be a breeze.

Launching the new process

The company launched GPS for all its headquarters and 'upper field' employees (regional directors and district managers) in January 2014, although the specifics of how the scheme was launched differed in each business unit. 'We identified implementation teams in each business unit to whom I handed the change plan, communication and programme materials and gave them the goal of achieving the behaviour changes in three years,' said Ollander-Krane:

> But we left it up to them how they wanted to do it. Some wanted to start with the philosophy, and they took a deep dive into the concept of growth mind-set with their employees and waited to talk about the specifics of the new process. Others jumped right in to all the tactics and the programmatic elements. Eventually they had to cover both sides, but we gave them the flexibility to drive it into their business unit in the way they thought would most resonate with their people.

Providing training and support

The team rolled out several learning modules at various times during the year to provide help and support with different aspects of the new process. In May 2014, it launched a module for managers on how to conduct more effective feedback conversations to coincide with the first 'touch-base' sessions. Then towards the end of the year it launched a class for managers on how to have an effective reward conversation and how to allocate bonuses using the new process, while everyone in HR received training in how to conduct a pre-calibration discussion with managers.

A positive response from HR...

The new process has had a clear and positive impact on the amount of administration HR has to carry out each year. Ollander-Krane said:

> At year end, under the old process, our compensation team would get a constant barrage of calls, asking them to solve problems and change ratings. It was really high pressure for them and they came to hate the end of the year. Even our senior vice president of HR would get 40 to 50 calls from senior leaders in the company who were disgruntled with their own outcomes – something in their review that they didn't agree with, for example, or that they didn't like where they had landed on the forced distribution curve.

The first year of GPS could not have been more of a contrast: 'At the end of the first year under the new process, the comp team said it was a non-event. The phones weren't ringing and the senior vice president of HR got one call instead of 50.'

GPS has also saved managers and employees a lot of time. 'Employees used to write pages to try and justify a high grade in their end-of-year review and managers would also spend days preparing for these discussions,' said Ollander-Krane. 'Now the end-of-year discussion takes no preparation for employees and limited preparation for managers. And it lasts just 10 minutes.'

... and from employees

Ollander-Krane ran several employee surveys throughout the first year of GPS, and these revealed a similarly positive response from employees. 'We don't ever want to be seen as the 'police' or to be monitoring people. But in the first year we did want to track whether or not the 'touch-base' conversations were actually happening,' he recalled.

A simple online survey was developed that went to every employee in the headquarters. It asked four questions. First: 'Have you had at least one touch-base per month for the last quarter – yes or no?' An impressive proportion of 90 per cent said 'yes'.

The second survey question asked: 'Are these conversations helping to increase your level of performance?' Employees had to rate the conversations on a scale of 1 to 5, with 5 being the highest. The average score turned out at 4.1. 'Again, that was really impressive,' said Ollander-Krane.

The third question was: 'Is your manager helping you to learn from your successes and failures and to apply that learning to the future?' The average score was 4.2.

The final question was: 'Does the way in which your manager gives you feedback make you want to get more feedback?' And again, it scored 4.2.

Ollander-Krane says: 'So we walked away from that survey feeling like we had a success on our hands.' Importantly, he adds, the team did not share these results with senior leadership or the rest of the business:

> We didn't do the survey for any disciplinary reasons or to say to senior leaders 'Look at who is doing well and who isn't doing well.' We only gave feedback to the managers themselves. It wasn't intended to be a formal assessment – it was meant to be a learning tool for us and for our managers, which fits really beautifully in a growth mind-set.

An opportunity for HR

Performance management has traditionally been owned by HR, and under the old process at Gap it was no different. Making wholesale changes and putting more onus on managers and employees to 'own' the process could have caused some consternation among the HR team, but Ollander-Krane says they have actually welcomed the new opportunities that GPS has opened up for them:

> We knew going into this that it would represent a big change curve for HR, as this is a place where HR has traditionally played a significant role. But we also knew it would be an exciting change for them – they would be going from policing the process, and just making sure people were following the rules, to acting as proper consultants.

So members of the HR team are still intimately involved in the process, but they are now spending their energy in a way that adds much more value. Ollander-Krane explains:

> Instead of just being there to ensure that the process is happening, they can actually coach managers in the best way to give feedback to their employees all year long. They can figure out the managers who are doing well and congratulate them and identify the ones who are struggling and help them improve. And they still play an important role in the calibration discussion with senior leadership – the only difference is that this now takes place ahead of the end-of-year reward meetings, rather than afterwards.

Reference

Taken from: e-reward (2016) *Performance Management Case Studies*, e-reward, Stockport

Appendix B

Performance management case study: Microsoft

Microsoft removes ratings and encourages collaboration

In 2013, Microsoft removed its previous system of performance management, which used a process known as 'stack ranking' to divide employees into five performance categories along a targeted distribution of ratings, and replaced it with a new approach to performance and development that emphasizes collaboration, feedback and rewards for impact. According to Lisa Dodge, Director, Global Performance Programmes, the change – now covering its 112,000-strong workforce worldwide – has brought positive results, with over two-thirds of employees and managers expressing satisfaction with the company's new approach in staff surveys.

A new company culture

Early in 2013, Microsoft began a journey to transform itself as a company – moving from operating primarily as a software developer to offering a much more diverse range of devices and services. This meant changing the structure of the organization and the way it worked. In particular, it required employees to embrace faster development cycles, be more accountable for their results and – most importantly – to collaborate much more closely with colleagues across the business.

The old approach to performance management

Under Microsoft's previous approach to performance management, individual performance was rated on a scale from '1' – the highest, to '5' – the lowest, in an end-of-year review. A targeted distribution required managers to work toward the specific distribution of ratings at different levels.

This led to difficulties. Managers and employees did not like the constraints. There was too much focus on where the employee had been rated on the distribution. People getting '3s' had done well and were well rewarded, but many felt upset or distressed to get a 'middle' rating.

What's more, it encouraged an unhealthy degree of internal competition and undermined teamwork between employees who knew there were only so many higher-level ratings to go around in an organization. Dodge says: 'It worked against collaboration, and it also got in the way of innovation and risk-taking.'

And the new approach to performance and development

The company's new approach to performance management is very different. In fact, Microsoft no longer refers to it as 'performance management' but rather 'performance and development'. As Dodge explains:

> The outcome of the old end-of-year review usually felt like a judgement, rather than an opportunity for employees to learn and get better. The focus of our current approach is designed to help people deliver great

impact by working together, reflecting and getting feedback more often, and more intentionally considering learning and growing – and as a result deliver continually better business results.

Dodge believes the previous approach tried to do too many things:

It was like a Swiss army knife of performance management – we were using it for everything from allocating reward to categorizing talent. The ratings people received became an overarching label of everything anyone in the company felt they needed to know about someone. And it became a gate to things – whether or not an employee could transfer, for example, or even whether or not they *should* transfer. It wasn't intentional, but it happened. And our employees didn't like it – which worked against the programme's ability to help improve performance.

In contrast, Microsoft's new approach was explicitly designed to meet three priorities.

1 Deliver results differently through teamwork

Microsoft adopted the idea of 'enterprise contribution' from consultants CEB, which suggests that employees can have the biggest impact on a business by combining their own contributions with the work, ideas and efforts of others.

This concept was the cornerstone of Microsoft's overhaul of its approach to performance management, framing how it now thinks about work and performance, how it has conversations about work and performance and how it recognizes and rewards people.

2 Feedback that helps you learn, grow and deliver results

Microsoft's new approach to performance and development abolishes performance ratings, the targeted distribution of ratings and end-of-year reviews. Instead, it encourages employees and managers to have several conversations each year that focus on the employee's impact and their learning, growth and development. The new process is designed to provide faster and more regular feedback. Dodge says:

We have removed distractions – like ratings and targeted distributions – that might get in the way of these good conversations. We've eliminated labels in favour of richer dialogue and feedback. And by encouraging people to talk more frequently, we hope to encourage them to reflect more often and then apply that learning more quickly to achieve increasingly better results.

3 Reward contributions to business impact

The new approach also brought a change by focusing more on business outcomes, and looking at the 'impacts employees have had'. The goal is to ensure that those making the greatest impact receive the greatest rewards.

Managers are more empowered to make reward recommendations for their employees within the new system – and, without the targeted distribution, they also have more flexibility in how they allocate rewards. The formal calibration process has been replaced with much lighter discussions around impact. Dodge says:

Our managers get together to focus on the individuals who have exemplified high impact within the organization, and to look at examples of low impact. The idea is to provide common standards and themes of high and low impact, using tangible and specific examples. Managers can then take these insights and use them to make adjustments to their initial recommendations before submitting them.

Regular performance conversations have been separated from the reward conversations. Instead of the end-of-year review, managers and employees have a short reward discussion to share the merit, bonus and stock outcomes with the employee. Meanwhile, the regular discussions employees and managers have during the year focus on the impact someone is having, what they are learning and what they can do in the upcoming few months – there is no discussion of rewards. Dodge says:

With the old system people were too distracted by their rating. Under the new approach, they are able to more fully appreciate their rewards... Our employees don't need ratings to know how they are doing... We want rich conversations rather than assuming an employee's performance can be boiled down to a simple label.

Connects

The regular conversations between managers and employees that form the core of the company's new approach to performance and development are called 'Connects'. Every employee is expected to have a minimum of two Connects a year; beyond this, Microsoft does not apply any strict rules. Some businesses even devolve it down to the team level, so each team manages them differently. Dodge explains:

> One of the key aims of the new system is that, other than reward –
> which we continue to do at one common time each year – we didn't
> want there to be any corporate-set rhythms around discussions. So
> we weren't going to continue the practice of mid-year or end-of-year
> reviews and we weren't going to tell people when to do their Connects.
> We just set the baseline minimum and then said that leaders and manag-
> ers would decide on when.

We told the leaders of each business to approach Connects in the way that made most sense for them. Some set a cadence – they say you need to have one Connect every four months. Others just say how many are expected over the course of the year and then they leave the details up to the individuals involved. And the number of Connects they have varies too. While some of our leaders have stayed at the minimum of two Connects each year, most have targeted three or four – and one team even has 12.

Framing the Connect conversation

To ensure managers and employees get the most out of their Connects, Microsoft developed a simple framework to help structure the conversations. Each Connect is centred on four questions, two of which look back and two of which look forward. A great deal of thought went into developing the four questions and the way they interplay, and into the psychological message the form conveys.

Employees and managers are expected to record their answers to these questions on a simple Connect form, which can then be submitted through an online system.

The two questions that look back at the employee's performance are: 1) What impact did you have? 2) What opportunities were there for greater impact? 'No matter how well people have performed, they should be able to answer those two questions,' says Dodge. 'And the second question really sets out the expectation that everyone can learn and do even better in the future.' The two questions designed to help the employees look forward are: 1) What are your upcoming deliverables? 2) What will you do to learn and grow in the upcoming period?

Along with these questions, employees are also expected to maintain a list of their core priorities. They are the overarching goals that people are trying to achieve. How people define their core priorities is very flexible. It is at the control of the employee – although managers' implicit agreement is still required.

An employee's core priorities might be relevant for three weeks, while another priority may be relevant for three years – or anywhere in between. Microsoft guides people to only have between three and five active priorities at a time and suggests that they only need to be two or three sentences long – they just need to describe what you are going to do, what the expected impact is and any ways to measure or quantify success.

Structuring the Connect process

In keeping with the flexible ethos of the new approach, how the Connect process is structured is left up to the individuals involved. By far the most common approach is for the employees to answer the four questions, update their core priorities and then submit the form to their manager. The manager may then add his or her comments but, before finalizing these, he or she will arrange to meet the employee to have a discussion.

Microsoft encourages managers to share their comments with the employee in advance of this meeting, so that there can be an effective two-way dialogue. After this, the manager finalizes his or her comments and submits the finished form. Then there are a few managers who choose to record their comments live during the discussion. The employee submits his or her answers ahead of time, but the manager does not write anything on the form until he or she is speaking with the employee.

Monitoring Connects

Because the process concludes with the manager posting a completed Connect form to the system, HR is able to see how many are being undertaken and where. Leaders and managers can also monitor this directly for their organizations or teams.

Scrapping ratings has reduced the fear and anxiety that employees felt in discussing performance, so people are much happier to take part in the process. Dodge says:

> The old distractions and internal competition have dramatically declined and both managers and employees indicate much higher levels of overall satisfaction. We provided a variety of training courses for managers on how to discuss performance without ratings and our employee surveys show that they are comfortable delivering a rewards message to their reports without ratings or any kind of year-end document.

Reward decisions

Despite removing performance ratings, the new approach to performance and development is still intimately tied to reward: a manager's decision on an employee's impact directly affects his or her salary increase, bonus and stock awards. In fact, managers now have even greater input to the rewards given to their direct reports. They make their recommendations by positioning a 'slider' for each employee along a continuum according to the amount of impact they feel he or she has had that year – and these recommendations are much more likely to be implemented than in the past, when the targeted distribution would sometimes lead to the manager's initial rating recommendation being changed, once the performance was compared to a broader group of employees.

However, while the targeted distribution of ratings has gone, managers are still expected to apply consistency and thought in their reward recommendations – and managers higher up the business review their decisions and ensure the total sum of all recommendations are within the prescribed rewards budget. It is only at the highest levels of the business that managers are expected to ensure they stay within their rewards budget. Managers lower down in the organization do not see these budget indicators, as Microsoft wants to avoid influencing their reward recommendations, recognizing that performance will vary between teams, and these smaller teams should not be expected to manage to budget but rather focus on their impact recommendations for each employee. Dodge explains:

> As a key part of the process, teams of people managers and their leader will meet for a 'People Discussion' where they share examples of higher and lower impact, ask each other questions, provide feedback and develop themes that help them with broader perspective when they consider their recommendations for other members of their team.

Talent management

Removing performance ratings does not only impact reward, of course – it also affects other important aspects of HR, such as talent management and succession planning. Dodge says:

> I don't want to overstate the role that ratings played at the company: they were never the sole determinant of succession planning, talent conversations or internal hiring decisions – they were just one input. But the ratings did offer a quick and easy way of – allegedly – seeing how a person had been performing over the past three years, and that felt easy and convenient.

The new approach requires a more in-depth view; for instance hiring managers need to read the Connect documents and have conversations with previous managers that provide better insights into an employee's performance and impact.

A positive response

The company has carried out lots of internal research, including several broad employee and manager surveys, to assess the impact of its new approach. The results show that it has been well received by employees and managers alike.

The percentage of employees who say they are satisfied with the company's approach to performance and development has increased from 50 per cent in 2012, under the old system, to 64 per cent in 2015 – while the percentage that are dissatisfied has fallen from 40 to 20 per cent. Managers' perceptions have improved even more – with those that are satisfied with the system jumping from 40 to 68 per cent, and the proportion who say they are dissatisfied falling from 45 to 18 per cent. 'We were thrilled with the results,' says Dodge. 'We didn't just move people from being negative about the system to being neutral – we actually moved them to feeling positive about it.' Perhaps most tellingly, the new system has also had a profound impact on people's perception of collaboration at Microsoft:

> They like the fact it has given them a lot more control and flexibility over their recommendations – and the outcomes no longer carry a label. They are no longer being forced to have conversations where they are telling people how good their performance was and that they are going to receive a good reward – and yet the employee just feels upset because they've been given a '3' rather than a '1'. It's mitigated so much of that threat, angst and distraction.

When Microsoft first raised the prospect of abolishing ratings and introducing a new approach to performance and development, there was some understandable unease, including by proponents of the idea – some were concerned that the top performers would not like it and would actually miss the ratings as they would be unable to differentiate themselves as clearly. 'We heard some concerns about potential unintended consequences of this change – even those of us close to this wondered about some of those same concerns. We were glad, a year later, to see data that busted those myths,' says Dodge.

In fact, satisfaction – especially among top performers – has increased. And there were some who felt that employees who received a typical reward outcome, somewhere in the middle of the range – a '3' under the previous scale – would still feel disenfranchised. But in fact, their satisfaction ratings increased from 45 to 67 per cent, while the proportion who is dissatisfied has dropped from 43 to 14 per cent. Satisfaction ratings are higher across all levels of reward. Dodge says:

> The only thing we have really looked at is continuing to refine some of the tools, resources and guidance we provide around the approach to continue building capability. But that really just falls under the heading of 'everything can always be better' – it's not because we have identified any particular problems or gaps in the design.

Dodge acknowledges there is still a way to go. A perennial issue remains that employees still lean more towards looking at their impact as an individual rather than thinking about how they have contributed to other people's work. 'But that is to be expected really. There is a long-rooted history of focusing on individual achievements here and it will not disappear overnight. But we've seen good progress and we're getting better all the time.' She adds: 'Real cultural change is a marathon. We're not just trying to change our approach to performance – we're trying to change mind-sets.'

Reference

Taken from: e-reward (2016) *Performance Management Case Studies*, e-reward, Stockport

INDEX

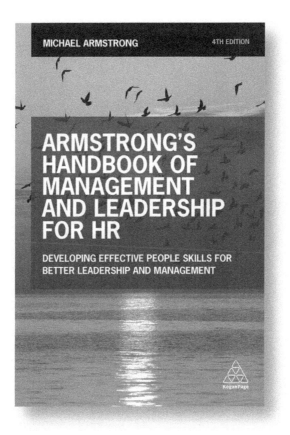

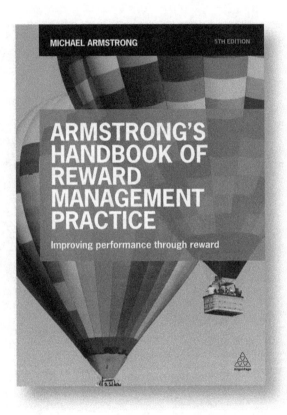

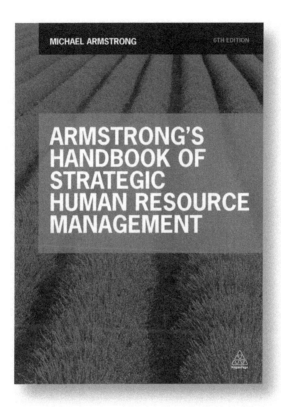

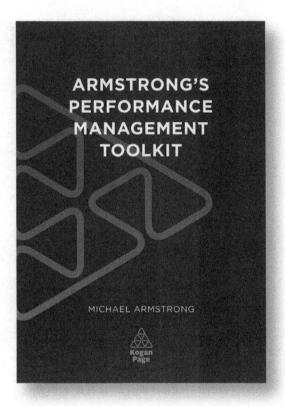

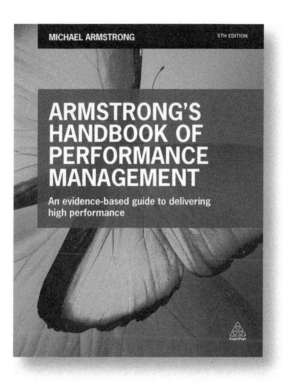